TO **GET PAID FAR MORE** THAN YOU'RE **WORTH!**

HOW TO GET PAID FAR MORE THAN YOU'RE WORTH!

Dr. Gary S. Goodman

MEDIA

MEDIA

Published 2019 by Gildan Media LLC
aka G&D Media
www.GandDmedia.com

Front cover design by David Rheinhardt of Pyrographx

Interior design by Meghan Day Healey of Story Horse, LLC

Library of Congress Cataloging-in-Publication Data is available upon request

ISBN: 978-1-7225-0195-2

10   9   8   7   6   5   4   3   2   1

Contents

Chapter 4

Mastering the Psychology
of Getting Paid More

Chapter 5

How to Transition into
Earning the Big Bucks

Afterword

You Are Invited!

Chapter 1

Do What You Love and Get Paid Ten Times More for It!

One of my favorite consulting stories goes back to a time when I was in Houston, helping a financial-services sales team to improve their training process.

One fellow was really struggling. He seemed to be doing everything reasonably well, but his results were a big pile of nothing.

The rep's inability to rack up any sales went on for about ten months, from January to November. Not only was it humiliating for him to watch others with less experience succeeding faster, but it was costly, because he was on a straight commission pay plan: he earned money only when he brought in business. No business meant that no money, zilch, *nada*, was earned.

Suddenly, one day in early November, his ship came in. A Japanese bank made a major investment in one of the seller's bond funds, and this hapless fellow wrote his first order. And that first sale brought him a $1 million commission.

This event raises the all-important question: was that rep paid an equitable amount? Was he underpaid, justly paid, or overpaid? Was he paid less than his worth, equally to his worth, or more than his worth?

From the rep's point of view, he earned every penny of the million bucks. After all, he agreed to take a job where the pay was completely contingent on sales, and it amounted to zero for the better part of a calendar year. He gambled and he won.

You know the expression: boats are usually safe in a harbor, but that's not why they're built. They prove their seaworthiness in choppy currents, storms, and battering conditions. Likewise, if you want to catch the bigger fish, you have to take one of these vessels far from shore, and there's no guarantee you'll catch one. Indeed there's no assurance you'll even come back in one piece.

This sudden Houston millionaire was at sea for a long time before he got a bite. He paid an uncertainty premium, investing in a job, a company, and products that might not have paid off. He could have hung around for another ten months, earning nothing. But he had a chance to get rich, and the opportunity penciled out. There were big dollars to be made, providing he applied himself and contacted prospects that could purchase big and were good for the money. If these things lined up, he had a shot.

You've heard that old quote from bank robber Willie Sutton. When asked why he robbed banks, he said, "Because that's where the money is."

If you want to be paid what you're worth, and especially far more than that, you'll need to go where the money is.

Can you work at McDonald's and discover gold?

Yes and no. If your focus is only on getting by, earning the wages they pay to new burger and fry flippers, then the answer is no.

However, many McDonald's franchisees came from the rank and file. They rose in the ranks to management and then arranged to get financing. Many multimillionaires have been made from McDonald's franchisees.

If you go back far enough, you'll see that Ray Kroc, the founder of the McDonald's empire, gave his loyal secretary stock that made her a multimillionaire. She was working with Kroc in his start-up phase. She got in early and stayed for the long haul.

This story is being repeated in Silicon Valley, Silicon Beach, and elsewhere every day. Money is everywhere. There's no shortage of it, except perhaps in your pocket or bank account. You need to see that as a temporary condition. You may have been born poor, but you don't have to stay that way.

It has been said that the biggest bankrupt in the world is the person who has lost enthusiasm. By this measure, if you are enthusiastic, you are already rich. It may take a while to financially cash in, but you will.

Dr. Srully Blotnick did some fascinating research. He studied a group of a few hundred people over twenty years. Some got rich and were paid more than they were worth. Others didn't.

What were traits of those that became wealthy? Were they more educated?

No, they weren't.

Did they all go into booming sectors like technology or financial services?

No, they did not. They got rich in all walks of life.

The common thread was that the rich folks entered a field that they loved and enthusiastically pursued. They remained interested in it over many years, and they became so good at their tasks that the world noticed their exceptional skill and quality.

Inevitably they outearned their peers from the study group. That extra money was put into investments that they allowed to grow.

Blotnick's slow but sure method can successfully transport you from rags to riches, although it isn't as dramatic as earning a million-dollar commission or cashing in stock options.

For these slowpoke millionaires, their net worth came as a surprise to them. They were not focused on money. They kept their eyes on a different ball, one that related to their personal interests. They immersed themselves in their fields, and the money followed.

Perhaps they wanted to become the best at what they did. Or they simply wanted to continually improve, to find better and better ways of doing what they loved.

Masters in most fields are paid more than the average practitioners, that's for sure. The best university professors—and by "best" I mean the standouts, those that contribute the most—can earn in the serious six figures.

Preachers with large and supportive congregations can live lavishly, enjoying perks such as spacious and well-appointed offices and homes. They can also be paid serious salaries and receive generous retirement plans.

If you are especially competent, you will succeed, and wealth will find you.

But most of us are interested in taking a faster flight to the promised land of prosperity. We want shortcuts, fast tracks.

Do they exist?

They do. Mostly you'll find the portal to being paid a superior amount is marked with the word *negotiation*.

Generally, in your career, you won't earn what you're worth. You'll earn what you NEGIOTIATE.

When most people think of negotiation, they imagine a bargaining table or an interviewing room. At some point after we say hello but before we leave, negotiation takes place.

But really negotiation begins long before the first offer is floated. It begins before the interview starts, and even a long time prior to when we were thinking of applying for a particular job.

Negotiation begins between our two ears, in our minds, when we formulate an intention to become someone or to get something.

When I was growing up, I was treated to a never-ending car show. My neighborhood was filled with pricey and exotic makes and models. A few blocks away, you could see a Lincoln, a Cadillac, a Mercedes, a Ferrari, and a Rolls-Royce idling at the same stoplight.

Thus my idea of a nice car started long before I was ten years old. To me, the epitome of a great car was a dark-red Bentley convertible. The one I wanted had white glove-leather interior with red piping and a tasteful burl dash with matching console. That was the model of my dreams.

That exact car became the benchmark for my aspirations.

Negotiation starts with setting an aspiration level. We aim at something. (More commonly, we aim at nothing in particular. And that's what we get.)

Back to my Bentley: that was not the first car I purchased, as you might imagine. My first was a very used VW Bug. If I hadn't been awarded a leadership scholarship in college, I could not have afforded that.

A dozen years later, I bought a convertible. It was a deep red Mercedes sports car, with palomino interior and a wood dash and console. My tastes had changed. I didn't want to drive a boat anymore!

I didn't bargain hard for the Mercedes. This was an "I deserve it!" purchase. It was a reward and the realization of an aspiration that started long before.

The dealer probably thought I was an easy sale. That would be correct. I had sold myself on a similar dream car long before I entered his establishment. No outside persuasion was required. Ready or not, I was buying. All he had to do was hand me the keys.

We walk around with default settings for many aspirations. Some want the same type of home that they grew up in. Parents want for their children the childhoods they had, or perhaps didn't have.

In some cases, our success settings come from what we think we deserve. If you believe, tacitly or explicitly, unconsciously or consciously, that you have no rightful claim to driving a Bentley or Mercedes convertible, how likely is it that you'll own one?

On the other hand, if you believe you are destined to drive such a fine machine, then will it be odd when it finds its way into your garage?

Aspiration levels produce elevation levels. You'll rise to or descend to the level of your expectations.

Right now, I'm at my desk with keyboard in lap. The beautiful waters of the Channel Islands, off the coast of Southern California, ebb and flow a few feet yonder. I see the wavelets, yachts, ducks scooting about, and a blue, billowy sky overhead. How did I end up here?

I used to go out to dinner at the beach, and I'd request a table with an ocean view. Sometimes I'd get it, and sometimes I wouldn't.

For a hoot, when I was eating at restaurants in Indiana or Ohio, I'd ask the host for a table "with an ocean view, please." Usually they'd laugh, and then they'd give me the best table in the house as my reward for lifting their spirits.

But there is something deadly serious about asking for an ocean view every chance you get. That is, if you really want to have an ocean view.

Make it known! Announce your intention! Tell the universe, as often as you can. The universe is listening.

More importantly, you and your subconscious are listening.

You're setting forth an ambitious aspiration. "I want this!" you're telling everyone, including those that cannot directly deliver it.

This, by the way, is not my first ocean view. I've had several, and I may have more. I have grown accustomed to having it, and I don't wish to settle for less! You might say what started as a luxury has now become a necessity, and I'm happy I said that.

This is the way it works with compensation. You'll earn what you absolutely *must* have. If you must have only some protection overhead, any bridge will do. That's fine, if you're happy with it, but you're reading this book because you want more. You want more than the average, correct?

I'll never forget quoting my consulting fee to a cynical fellow a number of years ago.

"Why, the average consultant only charges $1,500 a day!" he barked.

You know how I replied? "Well, I'm not average, and I believe you're looking for a consultant who is substantially above average, aren't you?"

Let's be clear with each other: you want to be paid far more than you're worth, right?

Companies Conspire to Underpay You

The world will tell you, repeatedly, that you're only worth average pay. This is expressed in many ways.

Commonly, corporations will claim to have done salary surveys. They'll say the range for the position they're seeking to fill is between $60,000 and $70,000 per year. By definition, if you want more, you won't be worth it. No one is, you see, because the survey says so. These wages are almost always less than what you need to have an above-average existence. We'll get into the specifics of breaking out of the stated salary ranges later.

Who Always Earns Far More than He Or She Is Worth?

This morning, I looked up a different salary range, which I'm sure you'll find interesting. It is how many multiples of the average worker's pay corporate CEOs earn.

According to Payscale.com, General Electric's CEO earns 139 times the average pay of GE's workers. That's $11,271,000 for CEO Immelt and $81,000 for the average Joe or Josephina. Honeywell's CEO earns 211 times the median pay. At Goodyear, life is good indeed for the CEO, who gets 311 times the average.

Would you say these individuals are earning far more than they're worth?

How much is too much?

And who is to say?

In the case of CEO pay, that decision is not made by the human-resources department. It is made by the board of directors. They may be chums of the CEO.

One of my points is to make you aware of the arbitrary and often exaggerated ratios between pay and performance in the employment sector. These CEOs are employees, just like the loading-dock worker and the mailroom clerks, but they're getting rich from their labor.

In every case, these CEOs are only given 168 hours per week. That's precisely the number you and I get. What says they should earn hundreds of times more than you earn? Are they that much better-looking? Are their IQs so much higher? Is their diploma, bachelor's degree, or MBA so much more awesome than yours? Did they select better parents? Did they win the swimsuit competition? Is their golf or tennis game that much more skilled?

The answer to all these questions is no. I would argue that they are not paid far more than the average person because they are so distinguished. Rather, their greatest distinction is simply that they are paid far more than the average person.

I'm not telling you to envy or to resent them. On the contrary: admire them! They cash those huge checks with a straight face. They sleep on clouds. Chefs serve them the tastiest and most nutritious fare. They have vacation homes in the best places, and they consort with others of their ilk annually at Davos, Switzerland.

People will treat you as you expect to be treated. You must see yourself in a different light to get different results and different treatment. You need to see yourself as these CEOs. Tell yourself you *are* them. Possibly you're even *more* than they are.

That's if you want game-show money or "I just won the lottery!" megabucks. It is possible to be paid far more than you're worth. These CEOs are proving it with each breath and private jet they take.

Don't Change Anything— Just Earn a Lot More!

For the purpose of an exercise, let's scale back your ambitions.

Maybe you don't want to work hard. In fact you want to do practically nothing other than what you're doing now. You simply want to be paid far more than you are being paid. How does that work?

You're ready for my *5 percent solution*.

I ask my trainees in negotiation seminars to imagine being merely 5 percent more effective in their negotiations. Of course they expected to get a lot more horsepower than a mere 5 percent gain. They want to double, triple, and quadruple their effectiveness.

I know this, and I don't rule out the possibility. I've seen tremendous leaps in income in short intervals. But let me remind you that big oak trees grow from tiny acorns.

Let's say you improve the yield from your compensation negotiations by 5 percent each year, compounded. Instead of getting $60,000 for that first position, you earn $63,000 or more. Plus you get 5 percent more vacation days, and 5 percent better retirement benefits.

You are 5 percent more effective on the spending side as well. When you purchase housing, transportation and everything else and you spend 5 percent less per year, what will happen? Over the course of a thirty-year career, you'll probably be wealthier by an extra million dollars. Remember that fellow that earned the $1 million commission? You'll be richer, I presume, from a tax standpoint. He had very few write-offs to diminish the huge tax hit he took.

Think Big and Act Small

You don't have to be a negotiation genius or make lopsided deals when you sell your services to earn far more than you're worth. Do just a little better every chance you get.

Herb Cohen wrote a book a while ago called *You Can Negotiate Anything!* He describes how he purchases a business suit. He'll go into a store and select one he likes. Then he'll call over the salesperson and ask him what he thinks.

The seller will feel he has a live one and will be very attentive. Then he'll try to close the deal:

"Let's have the tailor personalize this suit for you."

The tailor will chalk those spots where the item needs to be taken in and will put pins in the seams. Lighthearted banter will be exchanged, and everyone will be in good spirits. Cohen will then ask, "What shirts and ties do you think will go with this?"

Barely able to contain his excited anticipation at earning a big commission, the seller will dash to get the requested items. Cohen will make a great show of matching each to the suit. He'll remove the new garb and smile. Then he'll ask the seller, "You'll throw in a shirt and tie if I purchase the suit, right?"

What can the seller do—decline? At this point, the seller wants the sale, the tailor wants the sale, and they don't want to lose it.

Most sellers will agree to Cohen's "nibble," as he calls it.

In negotiation, a nibble isn't an entire meal. Cohen isn't asking for a twofer, two suits for the price of one. All he wants is what will amount to 5 to 15 percent improvement.

Cohen has calculated that if he only succeeds at a 5 percent improvement level, he is profiting at a higher rate than Fortune 500 companies do annually. The moral to the story is to ASK.

You don't need that much of an extra spiff to come out far ahead in the long run. That is, if you ask a lot, at practically every opportunity.

I'm choosing 5 percent as a goal. You could use this or select your own. You might be very successful upping the ante by 10 percent in salary negotiations. Or if you play one company's offer against another's, which I discuss in a different section, you could shoot for 20 percent or more.

Remember that every extra gain you rack up initially will be multiplied many times over the course of your career because of compounding. It pays, handsomely, to stretch that initial offer!

You might feel an aversion to Cohen's style. This is common. We've been trained to pay retail for what we get. We have been acculturated into accepting the finality of a price tag. It never occurs to most that the price of a retail item is negotiable.

Retailers love this about people. Like sheep, they'll pay pretty much what is asked of them. In the same way, employment seekers and income improvers accept what they are offered, without hesitation.

"It must be right," they think.

Price tags are very recent inventions. For tens of thousands of years, buyers and sellers got along very well without them. As is still the custom in many of the world's retail marketplaces, they'd make offers and counteroffers and then arrive at a price that suited both of them.

Do What You Love and Be Paid Ten Times as Much!

Speaking of careers, I started mine delivering and retailing newspapers as a kid. My first white-collar job was at eighteen. I collected past-due accounts for a finance company. I did a credible job because it was phone work. Nobody could see me. Endowed with a mature voice that had a bit of training in school drama and forensics classes, I could sound powerful and convincing on demand.

That voice has carried me quite a way. Next stop: Time-Life, where I became a top seller and manager. Then more selling while in grad school and a handful of years of college teaching—teaching others to use their voices persuasively. I was a top-rated teacher, wildly enthusiastic about my topic.

One day it hit me. But for the fact that my university was part of a consortium where I could enroll my children free of charge, on my teacher's salary I would not have afforded the tuition at my own school.

That seemed very unreasonable to me. Plus, in inflation-adjusted dollars, I was earning half of what I had earned at Time-Life eight years earlier.

Eight years before, I had completed no degrees.

I asked a critical question that I urge you to ask in relation to your own career interests:

How can I do what I love, which is teaching, and get paid way, way more than this university thinks I'm worth?

How much more did I want? I wanted triple or quadruple what I was earning, because I had already pulled down double in sales and management.

Let's say you are currently employed. You perform customer-service work, earning $50,000 per year. Are there ways you could still do that work while earning $150,000 or $200,000?

I want you to get creative here. Maybe, you need to enlarge what "customer service" means.

If it includes selling, then this income could definitely be yours. I understand that the root of the word *sell* is derived from the Scandinavian *selje*, which means *to serve*. So in that sense, selling is not a far cry from serving.

In my case, I wanted to continue my teaching, and I liked being affiliated with universities. I asked, is there a way I can teach at universities, yet be paid triple or quadruple what I'm earning? See how specific I was getting?

Sometimes the breakthrough comes by selling your labor differently.

I started questioning the very format of university teaching. Why was the teaching year from September to May, plus summer sessions? Why were we paid bimonthly? And if we taught larger sections, serving more students, shouldn't we earn a bonus? After all, there were more papers to grade and more demands placed on my time during office hours.

It was too late to rewrite my tenure-track teaching contract. But there was a way to address the mismatch between my efforts, my teaching gifts, and my compensation.

How I Became a Rich and Happy College Professor

I decided to try teaching in continuing education instead of in the undergraduate curriculum. There I could exert control over a number of factors. I could teach by the day, not by the semester or year. And I could charge a fee that vastly outstripped what I earned by teaching in the ordinary university curriculum. I could design my own seminars, programs that would attract business audiences.

Plus—and this was crucial—I could teach at multiple universities simultaneously. If one of them didn't offer a great wage, the next one could.

Becoming a day laborer, like the folks that troll for work outside the Home Depot, isn't exactly what professors willingly do. Yet I did the arithmetic, and it was promising.

Continuing-education programs paid $250–500 per day to those that taught business programs. I was earning less than $1,200 a month as a full-time assistant professor. If I could sell only five days a month as an itinerant teacher, I'd beat what I was pulling in. Plus I'd have a lot of free time. That could be used to develop new seminars or to do additional teaching dates.

My first engagement was during winter break. I returned to Los Angeles in January and we had six signups. So that program barely made.

Significantly, those that attended liked it and evaluated it highly. When I returned to the Midwest, I booked the program at Indiana State University. We did some productive publicity, and forty-four people enrolled. Because my subject was topical, the ABC-TV affiliate interviewed me at the scene. This added a bit of a celebrity buzz to the proceedings. It was also a reward for my sponsors, who had the good sense to develop a winner of a program.

I rebooked my class at ISU, which sponsored "tours." We did a number of dates throughout the region, and these succeeded as well.

I worked out an arrangement with various schools which guaranteed me a certain fee, but once we exceeded a certain number of registrants, I'd split every additional dollar of tuition with the school fifty-fifty. In many cases, this came to thousands of dollars per day. I added training materials and charged separately for those.

Because I wanted a change, and the income math was working out, I resigned my professorial post and dedicated myself full-time to this new venture. Within eighteen months, thirty-five universities were offering my programs, and some of these were doing it multiple times each year.

My income shot up almost immediately to about $150,000 per year. That was more than a tenfold increase from what my professorial pay had been.

Remember that question I asked: is there a way I can teach yet be paid three or four times what I was earning?

The answer was a resounding yes. I outstripped that ambitious goal by about three times. I was still associated with universities, which was a goal. Indeed, by being at thirty-five of them, arguably I had more prestige that I had being hidden from view at the liberal-arts school where I had been employed.

I also distributed my risk. When you work for one outfit, it is easy to get bogged down in the politics of that place. If you have a single enemy, or your boss isn't supportive, then going to work there every day can be hugely uncomfortable and unsatisfying.

I looked around at my faculty peers and saw about eight dour people that would inform the decision, seven years down the line, as to whether I would be granted tenure or meet a less desirable fate. I didn't trust them, or the chair of the department, to pass fair judgment. My instincts told me I wasn't going to win them over.

By starting my own university on the move, I'd avoid the politics of a single employer. Sure, there were politics associated with my short courses, but they were relatively easy to negotiate. Plus, if I didn't like a place or they didn't like me, it was easy to replace them. One school in thirty-five represented less than 3 percent of my teaching commitment. I could even lose half of my sponsors overnight, and I'd still be profitable. I could always invent a companion course and spend two days at a venue instead of one.

I expanded this way. Plus I rebooked my programs on an even tighter schedule, making them yield more income.

I launched my business, which was little more than teaching, with zero money. I only had my core skills and some credentials behind me, but they were enough. I marketed my courses by telephone. The first school that agreed to sponsor my seminar was in Los Angeles.

A phone call started that relationship. When I got back to Indiana, I used the free telephone line in my office to contact more schools.

Recall how my career started: I sold newspapers. Then at Time-Life Books, I sold their volumes over the phone on a subscription basis. I've been in the information and knowledge business my entire life!

Assess Your Skills and Cash Them In Big-Time

You need to assess your skills. For me, it has boiled down to leveraging the written and spoken word. I'm a talker and a writer.

You could use those gifts to ask, "Want fries with that?" or to ask, "How could we bring my seminar to your campus?"

You're using the same skill set. You're communicating. You're persuading. You're asking someone that has the power to purchase to do just that, to exercise it for your mutual betterment.

One expression of that skill will earn you a minimum wage. Another will earn you a six-figure income and make you a millionaire. The Bible tells us not to cast your seeds onto sand. To me, this means pick your shots. Be selective in deploying your gifts.

How selective are you right now? Are you being paid far more than your skills are typically worth?

If you aren't in a circumstance where you are leveraging your personal strengths and career assets, find another. If you seek out better places and become convinced they don't exist, don't give up. Create the circumstances you want, following my humble example.

Again from the Bible: "Ask and it will be given to you; seek and you will find; knock and the door will be opened to you."

Ask the right questions.

"What are my best skills?"

"Where can I apply them and earn multiples of what I'm currently earning?"

How can you recognize your best skills? Ask these questions:

"What comes easily to me?"

"What is supereasy for me to do, although others find it hard?"

The telephone is one of my chief sales and marketing tools. Don't get me wrong. I still have some butterflies in my stomach as I start to make calls, especially when I'm doing a new campaign and I have no track record. When I made calls to the first two university sponsors, I was riddled with fear. I hadn't done any selling for months, because I was writing my doctoral dissertation and then teaching. Nor did I have any clue to the reception I'd get to my new course idea. Would they gruffly reject me? Would they pity me and lead me on, having no intention to become sponsors?

But these fears were easily overcome. I reminded myself that I was good and capable over the phone. Relative to most others, I had very little phone fear. Indeed I always calmed myself with the idea that picking up the phone was a lot easier than driving to see someone, and it was far more efficient.

So this is a definite skill, and it continues to assist me in my career. There are days when I make fifty to 100 cold calls.

Let's look at another skill. Let's say you remain utterly calm in the face of others who could be screaming at you, hurling epithets that would make most people cringe or flee. Currently you're doing customer support, earning slightly more than minimum wage. But again, you're uncannily effective at calming people down and saving customers. How can you be paid far more than you're worth for this skill?

There are at least two proven ways to give yourself a huge raise. Let's say you're working in a field where the item that has offended people is relatively inexpensive. A light bulb burns out within weeks of service, and not months or years, as promised by the warranty.

The company that employs you cannot spend $15 solving a $5 problem. It is simply not economical. So your current firm *must* pay you a low wage, because there is so little at stake.

Do you see what I'm talking about? Your ability to calm people down outclasses the product you're representing.

You need to go upscale.

Forget light bulbs! Think designer goods, where there are huge profit margins, from which you can earn higher wages.

The lifetime value of a light-bulb customer could be—what, $250 or $500?

What is the lifetime value of a collector of designer handbags that retail for several thousand dollars apiece? That person's value could be in the hundreds of thousands or millions of dollars to a designer label or upscale store. Allowing that sort of person to be enraged or even mildly upset is very expensive.

This is where you enter the picture with your marvelous calming capability. Now you are a huge asset and an incredibly valuable part of the business. Justifiably, you can earn multiples of what you were paid to deal with light-bulb customers. Save a designer-goods client and you've saved a lot of income, and you're worth part of that income.

The second way to ply your exceptional skill in calming people is to become a mediator. While lawyers, retired judges, and psychologists perform this function, with many types of mediation you don't need licensing. If you charge $500 to $15,000 per consultation to dampen a dispute, you'll be worth every penny, depending on what is at stake.

Your skill is exactly the same as it was in the light-bulb customer-service unit.

Pardon me if I say it's a lot brighter to apply your skill in a more enlightened setting!

How to Multiply Your Income Streams
Better applications of your skills lead you to even better opportunities.

I expanded my college training business organically. One college sponsor became two, and two became thirty-five. One course became two and then four courses, when you include the spinoffs and management versions I created. On top of that, I became a best-selling business author and audio entrepreneur. These good things came about because I had massive exposure through thirty-five course catalogues across the country.

I was being discovered by great resources without being aware of it.

Specifically, the giant business-book publisher Prentice-Hall/Simon & Schuster called a very small university where I was teaching a seminar. An editor left a message asking me if I wanted to write a book.

I replied, "I'll do better than that; I'll write two."

By that time I was doing two seminars, so I felt it was natural to sell two manuscripts simultaneously. As it turned out, I churned out six titles in five years. Four of them went on to best-seller status. The widespread distribution of these volumes attracted corporate sponsors: companies that sought to bring me in to train their people.

I was multiplying my marketplace presence through books, publicity, live seminars, and onsite training programs. I also started to do a number of convention speeches quite successfully. I published my own audio versions of seminars as well. So there were several expressions of the same content, as well as elaborated and customized versions. I was also starting to benefit from passive income from book royalties on top of active income streams from my other exposures.

I call this "dimensionalizing" a product line. One offering becomes several, and each buyer can purchase multiple layers of products and services. College-class attendees can purchase a book or tape and recommend me as a speaker to their company or professional association.

This is definitely a way to be paid far more than you're worth. There are lots of others.

Build More Value and Earn More Value in Return

The more value you create, the more of a right you have to share in that value.

For example, I developed an original product line in the customer-service area. It contained unique practices for enhancing customer satisfaction. I also developed a unique set of performance measurements that enable managers and service reps to evaluate achievement and customer satisfaction.

To deliver these benefits required a lot of on-the-clock training and coaching as well as development time.

Let's say a company had twenty people to work with. It might require thirty contact days, or six full weeks of training, to create results.

Thirty days aren't cheap from a billing standpoint. In some cases, my contracts ran to hundreds of billable days at a given company, resulting in substantial six-figure agreements.

The more value I created, the more money I got.

Chapter 2

Eureka! How to Cash In the Big-Money Value of Your Skills

There was always an unstated concern among my customer-service improvement sponsors that they were paying a lot for please and thank-you training—a superficial program that they could purchase anywhere from anyone.

I responded by spending a lot of time and effort asserting my uniqueness. But this was the wrong way to go about being paid far more than I was worth.

Then I noticed a very happy accident. When customer-service reps would apply my call path to conversations, transaction times were significantly shortened. It took less talking time to get even better client results than were being garnered before. Conversations were both shorter and better.

Someone else in my position might have found this curious or mildly interesting, but I sniffed a competitive advantage. From the fact that conversations were shorter, I inferred that I could do larger and more profitable programs immediately.

You see, average call length is a widely used metric in customer-service centers. Managers are constantly trying to find ways to abbreviate calls. But they approach the challenge crudely. They tell their reps to speed up the rate at which they speak. This makes reps less comprehensible, and they're asked to repeat what wasn't understood.

This approach *lengthens* calls!

My method introduced a proverbial stitch in time that saves nine. Reps could sound relaxed and not rush. Calls seem luxurious, yet they are definitely 20 to 30 percent shorter than before. A shorter call equals greater efficiency. When we translate the savings into dollars and cents, costs plummet.

If you have a call center with 100 people, you can now handle the same call volume with 75. If you are growing, you can handle 125 percent of the call volume you have been doing. That's a net saving of 25 seats times $100,000 per seat, when wages and benefits and overhead are factored in.

If I could reduce call length by 25 percent in a 100-seat center, I would save that client $2.5 million in the first year alone!

How much can you charge if you are saving a company $2.5 million? Should you be paid 20 percent of the savings? That would be a half-million dollars. Thirty percent would bring you $750,000.

Let's go back a bit.

Before I made this discovery, I was used to charging by the day or by the class. There is a natural limit to what you can bill by the hour, day, or single event. But now I was morphing into billing *by creating a specific result*. That was the substantially shorter call.

I wasn't selling more polite customer-service reps, nor was I selling happier customers. Yes, these outcomes would occur as a result of my training, but these benefits were suddenly *free of charge*. They were bonuses on top of the savings that I was charging for.

I was now charging by what I saved the company in customer-service labor and overhead costs.

I found I could sell huge programs, *and there was no practical limit to what I could charge.* This was a true breakthrough. It became yet another way to be paid far more than I was worth.

But what sort of breakthrough was it? For one thing, I wasn't in the training business or the speaking business or even the customer-service business. I was in the cost-reduction business. Cost reduction is one of two ways for companies to profit. The other way is to sell more effectively.

Being in the cost-reduction business enabled me to make a powerful case before chief financial officers. These are the generally tightfisted, pragmatic, and even cynical individuals that are in charge of a company's purse. If they are on your side, it can make all the difference in selling a program. As a bunch, they don't care about glamour or flash or glitter, unlike some corporate fad purchasers, who want, for example, the big-name speaker for an event.

Plus I had no competitors. For a while, no one else could do what I was doing. They didn't have the knowledge. They were making calls longer.

If you're in a monopoly position, you need to know two things. First, you can charge practically anything you want for your product or service. Second, monopolies never last. Sooner or later, someone will knock you off. You'll attract imitators, code breakers, and spies that will try to do your act and undercut you in price.

But for a while, you will be riding the crest of your innovation.

What's really crucial to appreciate is that I was doing what I had always done. But now I was being paid far more than what I was worth!

I was a professor and taught at universities. By changing departments and course formats and audiences, I still taught at universities. But I was paid ten times and even more to do it.

I was doing customer-service training before I discovered how to bill for it creatively. Then I was able to charge ten times and more what I had been charging. But I was still doing customer-service training!

You see the pattern, right?

Same Gary, more money! Same activities, more money! Same talents, more money!

You can do it too.

The first step is to state a clear goal. Putting it in money terms is helpful. If you're making $50,000, imagine tripling it to $150,000. The next step is to ask, "What will it take to triple my income?"

I had a paper route when I was a kid. I delivered the news for the *Herald Express*. But there was a second paper in town, the *Citizen News*.

I was ambitious, so I contacted that paper. I asked if the same route I was covering for the *Herald* was available for me at the *Citizen News*. It was, and I nearly doubled my income on the spot.

At first keeping the two subscriber bases clear in my mind was quite a task. On more than one occasion a *Herald* customer received the other paper on her doorstep. My handlebars were twice as heavy to manipulate, but it was worth the extra effort.

My Clone and His Value Billing

When was I touring with one of my seminars, a fellow who worked at AT&T saw my act in Ohio and decided to become my clone. I'll call him Richard.

He quit his day job and became a consultant in my topical area. We would run into each other at conventions, and he reminded me that I trained him on one of my tours.

I think Richard was trying to show up the master by sharing the following story with me. What he was really doing was showing how a clever person can multiply his income.

"Gary, have you ever noticed getting inquiries from consulting prospects that ask you what you charge and then disappear after that?"

"Well, that happens," I replied. "Some people kick tires without having any serious intention to buy."

"But Gary, have you ever noticed that happens a lot to you with prospects in Ohio?"

"Not especially," I said.

Then he told me about his grand strategy. "Sometimes I've encouraged people to call you to get a quote, knowing you'd come back high. I knew I could count on you to quote a daily rate about three times higher than mine!" he beamed.

Then he asked me what I charged per day. I said about $3,500 on multiple-day contracts.

His charge was only $1,200: about a third of mine.

"How can you get away with charging only $1,200 a day?" I asked him in genuine amazement.

He went on to explain that out of five billing days, he might be at a client's site for only one. During the four that he was not present, he was doing multiple things for multiple clients. They all thought he was working full-time on their projects, but he may have been dedicating a half-hour to an hour to them. Because he was out of sight, no one was the wiser.

I was on site about four days out of every five, so it was clear that I was dedicating 100 percent of that time to them.

My competitor was bringing in more money for the same calendar time. He could charge five clients for the same day.

I met with considerable price resistance. Using me as a point of comparison, Richard practically eliminated price as an objection, opening a world of business that I would never get at my stated rates.

Richard went on to say that the development of a customized workbook could take him an hour to assemble, because it only required changing a few pages from a boiler-plated format. He might charge five days for that item, or $6,000.

This was the value of receiving a workbook pertinent to his projects. Richard was not duty-bound to radically discount the price of the item because a former client or clients had subsidized its creation. As long as former clients had not bargained with Richard for an exclusive on the workbook, he was free to reuse the generic portions and to bill for them.

When I heard this story, frankly I was shocked. It seemed deceptive as heck. But over the years I've come to admit that there was really a stroke of genius at the basis of his billing methodology. In fact this is called *value billing*, and it is an accepted and widely practiced way of earning far more than you're worth.

Clients are obsessed about getting the lowest possible rate for most things. They'll dicker for cars and houses whenever and wherever they can. But they'll apply the same hardball tactics to negotiating human services such as consulting. They're asking for trouble when they do this.

For one thing, there are qualitative differences between providers of services. In my estimation, I was at least three times more effective than my Ohio competitor. Thus my higher fees were justified.

But Richard recognized that a low price signals value to many undiscriminating purchasers. They placed a great deal of emphasis on comparing consultants by the daily rates they charged. Consequently, when there was a huge price differential, most average buyers thought I couldn't be that good and he couldn't be that bad.

He exploited this advantage. It was a shell game. You know that game of chance where a pea is placed under one of three walnut shells? Richard arranged his income so that clients thought the pea was under the $1,200 shell, but it never was. He distracted them from looking in the right place. The pea was hidden in plain sight under the "daily time" shell. How much time constitutes a consulting day? This is the question no one asked him. A "day" for him could be ten minutes or ten hours, depending on what he wanted to provide, at least when he was off-site.

No one ever thought to ask, how many clients are you selling that same day to? They tacitly inferred that one day went to one client only.

No consultant could put more than twenty-four hours into a day. But Richard did!

Clients could have avoided his exploitation by setting up a different formula for his consulting. They could have negotiated a flat fee for services. That would have made his off-site clock time irrelevant. It would have been a way to pay for results only, although that's not a perfect system either.

He was earning more than I was, but even more significantly, he was closing a lot more business than I was closing.

This was Robert's way to earn far more than he was worth. He knew consulting buyers were unduly fixated on the daily rate of billing. He gave them what they thought they wanted, which was an unbelievably cheap fee.

This story leads us to a very important question: *how are you going to charge for your labor?* Richard found a way to make more money than me by seeming to charge one-third of my rate.

He was betting on the relative value clients would perceive after having called me. He was basing his pricing on a fundamental economic truth: demand for most things is determined by price. If you can reduce price, you'll typically increase demand. This is called the *price elasticity of demand.*

Few companies will gladly pay a consultant $3,500 per day. It is usually the larger ones, the Fortune 1000. They are the ones that typically purchase the largest and most cutting-edge programs.

But there are over 25 million small businesses in the United States. They'll never cost-justify $3,500, but $1,200 isn't a big stretch for them. They believe they can afford that.

So my competitor opened his consulting practice to a huge universe of buyers. Moreover, he opened it to a very large population of Ohio and Midwest buyers, where he was located. He pared travel expenses by focusing his efforts on locals.

I was running myself ragged by consulting everywhere. It was typical for me to hop a plane in the middle of the afternoon on Sunday and return the following Friday night. Usually I was not able to bill for my travel time, so it ended up being "donated" from the $3,500 days I was billing for. Over the years, my regimen proved so exhausting that I would remove myself from the road for months and even years at a time. This resulted in lots of mini-retirements from nationwide consulting.

I got a lot done during those sabbaticals, but they were costly. By comparison, my competitor restricted his consulting practice to a small region that he could cover without breaking a sweat. *His system was sustainable on top of being more profitable!*

One of my clients was the maker of Super Glue. You know this product by the commercials showing a burly, hard-hatted construction worker dangling from a beam in midair. Before Super Glue was invented, consumers didn't have access to high-grade adhesives in small quantities. We had Elmer's Glue, a white, pasty stuff still used in classrooms for cut-and-paste projects. Model airplane glue was also available, but it could cause headaches and worse. Super Glue was a breakthrough that a chemist developed when he worked at a large company. He bought the rights and opened his own firm. He expressed his marketing goal this way: "Price it by the drop, but sell it by the gallon!"

My competitor found a way to do this with his clock time. He sold it by inexpensive drops, which looked cheap to buyers. But he sold gallons of those drops by allocating them in a creative way when he was off-site and out of sight.

When I had finished my PhD and was teaching at the liberal arts university I mentioned, I saw an article in the *Chronicle of Higher Education* about an esteemed graduate of my university. He had gone on to distinguish himself in the public-relations field, and he was based in Los Angeles.

I wanted to get to know him and hear his advice, because I was also in communications, and he was already rich and famous. He graciously agreed to see me at his office during the winter break, when I offered my first public seminar.

I asked him about his clientele, which included large utility companies and prominent corporations. It seemed his client list went on forever. Yet other than himself, only two or three junior staffers were on his team.

How could so few people satisfy so many large and demanding clients? Being the novice I was, I would have been thrilled to have only one of his dozens of patrons. He said he billed on a retainer basis. For a flat fee of say, $10,000 per month, a client would have access to his firm and specifically to him.

"But that spreads you pretty thinly, doesn't it?" I asked.

He just smiled. I pressed the point because I really wanted to know how he could manage competing demands for his time.

In the back of my mind was the health-club sub-scription model. Gyms and dance studios sign up a lot of people in January. These folks have made a resolution to get back into shape. The philosophy of the ownership is typically, "The more the merrier!" They won't limit sign-ups. But if you have oversold the capacity of your venue, what if all of the members show up at the same time? Won't you have a rebellion to quell?

The owners know this: with the best intentions, peo-ple make their resolutions and then fail to stick to them. A large proportion may try the place once or twice, but they'll find excuses to not use the facilities. Yes, they'll surrender a certain amount of prepaid dues, but they'll hold the gym harmless. Likewise, if they come at a time when there are two or three people waiting to get on an exercise machine, they'll blame themselves for arriving during peak hours.

There is research that predicts that a proportion of a population will flee under conditions of crowding. This will reduce the congestion. *So overselling the venue will actually introduce a corrective device. This will encourage you to keep overselling.* The gyms never disclose how many subscriptions they've sold, so there is no real account-ability.

I was asking this public-relations guru the same question. "What would you tell a client who asked you to account for the specific number of hours you invested working on his account during the month?"

He replied, in a very calm and reassuring manner, "I'd say 'I'm thinking about you all the time.'"

You have to love this answer for a number of reasons. For one thing, he shifted the ground of the question. I asked, when can you prove you *have* worked on their projects? He replied that there is never a time when he has *not* worked on their projects. You cannot prove a negative. If clients are uppermost in his mind all the time, they should be grateful that he isn't charging them even more.

On a practical level, do you hire a person of this stature to spend time and money accounting for that time and money or actually doing the work he is being paid to do? It would be penny-wise and pound-foolish to reduce this giant of public relations to the level of a bookkeeper or an account clerk, wouldn't you say?

I asked him if the unused time he was reserving was carried over from month to month, somewhat the way that unused cell-phone minutes are still yours as you move through billing periods.

Again, he smiled and simply shook his head.

That answer made sense. It was consistent with the idea that he thinks of each and every client all the time. If so, then by definition, how can there be unused minutes, hours, days, and months? They're all consumed, all the time.

Law firms have used a creative approach to accounting for the time they invest working on certain accounts. In most cases, they bill by the hour. That is expected and understood. But what happens when a firm agrees to write a letter on behalf of a client? Certainly this takes time, but how much? If the firm has written many letters of this kind, they have templates already set up. It could be a matter of simply filling in the name and particulars associated with the case at hand. Very little original writing is called for.

Let's say it takes thirty minutes to customize that letter, stamp it, and mail it? The firm charges $300 per hour. Will it bill a half hour? Will it invoice $150 for that letter?

No. That letter may be priced at $500 or $750 or even $1,250. Much like my competitor in Ohio, law firms nearly everywhere will assign a certain number of billable hours to the completed task, irrespective of the actual clock time invested in its completion.

What is the justification? I could give you a short reply and say "profit." But that would be simplistic.

Let's delve further into what is required to craft that letter. You're probably going to compose it while sitting in an office. That requires that the rent and utilities be paid. You have staff to pay and malpractice-insurance premiums to meet. You have to receive some compensation for your time to pay your living expenses. You may have student-loan debt and a lot of it. Law school wasn't cheap. You need a return on your knowledge and your investment.

Furthermore, how do you know *which* letter to send out, which one will be suitable for this client at this time? This requires expert judgment, and there are consequences if you choose incorrectly.

But I haven't asked an even more essential question: how much is that letter *worth* to the client?

You've been lost in the desert, and you're parched and hallucinating. Disoriented, you think you see a mirage, but it is really a vendor's stand. Though blurred, the sign reads, "Ice-cold bottled water."

You can't believe it. You might actually survive this ordeal?

You croak out the question, "How much for a bottle of water?"

The vendor says, "We do value billing here. How much is a bottle of water worth to you?"

That's a pretty good question, you must admit. Let's consider it carefully.

Well, you are thirsty, so it will be refreshing and it will taste good. What have you paid for water in the past: one dollar, sometimes two? It's certainly worth that.

But hang on. You don't just want that water. Your survival depends on it!

You have to have it!

Now calculate its value to you here and now. Do you have the power to say no? Can you refuse to buy it?

Of course you can, but that would be self-destructive. You'll perish if you do anything other than what's rational in the circumstance. That water is worth every penny in your pocket, isn't it?

In fact if the vendor says, "This costs $10 million," that's OK too, as long as you can reply, "Bill me! I'll pay you later!"

In other words, there is no limit to the value of that water to you, because your very life depends on it. You'll promise to pay $10 million later because without the water there will be no "later." You'll survive to worry about later, later.

Value billing is an attempt by buyers and sellers to calibrate the cost of a good or service according to its contribution. Implicitly or explicitly, all compensation formulas are trying to emulate value billing. The expression, "You get what you pay for" symbolizes this striving for equity.

Hourly billing and monthly and yearly salaries are shortcuts to establishing value. But they're distorted, and what is paid seldom dovetails perfectly with what is contributed.

Employers strive to pay so little that they won't lose even if they hire a dolt, a dud, a dolittle, or a ne'er-do-well. Employees seek the highest possible wages to pay for a decent lifestyle and as a premium to insulate against employer fickleness and irrationality.

Let's say you are the first employee hired by a new business. You're taking a big risk. Most businesses fail within a few years, so there is a good chance you'll be out on the street in short order, but for a while you'll be essential to the success of that firm. You'll be asked to wear multiple hats and to do various things. Indeed you'll be called on to do practically anything and everything to assist that fledgling to survive.

Let's say you succeed. Profits are created. More employees are hired, and you are cloned. Others do what you did so well. What are you worth?

In the beginning, they couldn't pay you enough, partly because they didn't have the money. You had high worth, and perhaps you were irreplaceable. Now they don't want to pay you what you were worth then, because they've distributed your duties to cheaper clones.

Your value has dissipated. And they diminished it on purpose, not wanting to be beholden to a mere employee.

When exactly can a person in your situation perform value billing?

You need to do it right away if you are joining a new enterprise. It is being done every day in places like Silicon Valley, Southern California's Silicon Beach, and elsewhere.

People just like you are bargaining for equity—partial ownership of the business.

It could be in the form of stock options that will vest after so many months or years of service. You will be given the right to purchase a certain number of shares in the company at a preset price. When the company prospers, the share price increases. Banks will lend you the money to cash in when your shares vest.

Let's say your options are for a $10 share price and you can buy 5,000 shares. The price goes to $50. At that point your options are worth about $250,000.

The proportions can be even more lucrative. If your company stock soars to 50 times its value, you're worth $2,500,000.

You can get rich working for other people, so the adage that says it is impossible is dead wrong. As we have seen, if you become a CEO, you'll probably get rich that way.

Being paid minimum wage isn't fun, and it certainly won't make you rich. But if you get equity as well, then that depressed wage may be temporary. Equity enables us to be paid far more than we're worth. Ask any long-term employee of Apple Computer who was issued stock options.

So far we've seen there are several ways to be paid far more than you're worth. I gave you personal examples of how I turned teaching into a far more lucrative career. I was also able to associate with universities, which I love. And I still have long-lasting teaching ties to UCLA and to UC Berkeley. These have been very gratifying to me. I was able to leverage my customer-service training programs into disproportionately more lucrative endeavors. I did this by charging based on the savings I was producing instead of focusing on selling the advantages of "please and thank you" training itself. Again, I did what I loved but was simply paid a lot more for doing it.

I've written at some length about setting your aspiration level to a higher point. This is what you strive for. Expect to excel, and visualize earning three and four and even ten times what you are earning now.

Announce your aims in creative ways. I kept repeating the fact that I wanted a table with an ocean view even at landlocked restaurants. Now I have one at home for all of my meals if I wish.

We discussed that corporate CEOs typically earn 100–300 times the average employee's earnings at their companies. They are the poster children for folks that are paid far, far more than they are worth. To think these CEOs are cut from a different cloth than we are is to make a critical error. They are the same. And if they can do it, so can you!

I've also mentioned my 5 percent solution. If you can negotiate only 5 percent more effectively, this can easily make you a millionaire over the course of your career. (We'll turn our attention to specific negotiation techniques in later chapters.)

We spoke about ways of suddenly earning windfalls of money. My favorite example is that investment seller who made a million-dollar commission from his first sale. He was able to stay on task after months of earning no money because he did the math of success. He knew if he applied himself, he'd earn a lot of money, more than he had ever been worth.

We've also spoken at length about selling your labor in creative increments, and how some people have been able to charge two-thirds less for their time but actually be paid far more than they're worth.

I've done these things. Others have and are doing these things too. Soon it will be your turn.

In the next chapters I'll show you specific techniques for getting paid far, far more than you're currently worth!

Chapter 3

The Art of Negotiating a Much Better Deal for Yourself

You Won't Earn What You're Worth—You'll Earn What You Negotiate

When I was selling for a financial firm, there were about a dozen others who were doing the same. Each of us was paid at a different rate. I had a guaranteed salary. To earn commissions, I had to beat a certain quota. Others were paid on a straight commission basis. One fellow earned a much smaller salary than I did. Why were there so many different versions of pay?

Everyone negotiated a different deal with management upon being hired.

I knew what my "nut" was: the amount I had to crack to make my expenses. I pegged some of my pay to that benchmark, and I added a hefty premium on top of it. This was to make sure I didn't have to break a sweat to break even.

I followed two of the Best Practices in Negotiation that I teach in seminars and my book *Dr. Gary S. Goodman's 77 Best Practices in Negotiation*:

1. If you don't ask, you don't get.
2. If you ask for more, you'll get more.

These are simple yet powerful precepts.

Let me share a secret with you. Most people fail to negotiate their salaries and perks. They don't even try!

This is more than stupid. It is self-destructive. They lose a ton of dough and other goodies by defaulting in this area. We're going to change that.

You *will* negotiate, even if you've never done it before. By simply *asking*, you get more than you even imagined possible.

Women are worse than men in failing to ask for what they want or need. This is documented. They ask about half as often as men. This puts them at a distinct disadvantage, which lasts for an entire career, and it costs them dearly. Let's say you're in a job interview and the person across the desk says, "This position pays $70,000."

This offer is the *least* they think you'll accept. It isn't the result of scientific study or a tremendous amount of intellectual noodling.

They looked at your application. You put down that you are used to earning $82,000. They won't start there. This means you should start at least 20 percent above what you want or will accept.

That is Best Practice number two above. The more you ask for, the more you'll get.

Of course, they're operating from the opposite end: The less they offer, the less they'll pay. We can "awfulize" all day and all night about the silliness of this bargaining game. We can agree it would seem so much easier to just cut to the chase. But negotiation does not work this way, and it never will!

Example: Some years ago, GM developed a lineup of cars called the Saturn. With much hoopla, GM opened showrooms and announced that Saturn would usher in a new era of the no-haggling dealership. The sticker price would be the sales price, period.

At first this seemed like a revolution. Car dealers were the few places where average folks thought they could and were even expected to bargain for what they paid.

But Saturn and its no-haggling format failed. As it turned out, you could outlaw haggling, but it would still happen. Most curious was the fact that a lot of consumers actually missed it.

You may hate negotiating. A lot of people find it uncomfortable. That doesn't surprise me. They don't get much experience! How frequently do we buy cars at dealerships? Once every five years might be the average. Let's say you negotiate once in five years, while car dealers negotiate every hour of every day, seven days a week. Who will do better in a bargaining session? The one with the ocean of experience compared to your droplet will drown you, right? You'll be out of your depth.

Unless, that is, you are highly prepared. Then you have a chance to improve your results.

I'm going to extend this car-buying example because it applies to getting paid far more than you're worth.

Dealers don't simply beat you on the price you'll pay for the new car. They actually have five or more profit centers. In addition to the new car's price, they'll earn profits on the used car you trade in, the financing you take from them, the extended warranty and other add-ons they'll pitch you, and on the equipment they'll pre-install on your new car and charge you for.

Those that pay your salary have similar profit centers, which will help them to make a superior deal if you are ignorant of these things.

Your salary seems straightforward, right? They'll pay you $5,000 per month. But you'd be smart to ask to be paid $1,250 per week, if it's all the same to them.

You can tell them your bill paying is budgeted that way. If they agree, you have just significantly upped your money, significantly.

There are 4.333 weeks in the average month, not 4. By getting them to pay weekly, you've improved their offer to $5,416.25 per month. That is an increase of $416.25 per month and a whopping $4,995 per year.

That puts you only $5 away from being paid for 13 months per year instead of 12!

This trick may not work with the biggest employers, whose pay periods are set in stone. But I've been the beneficiary of this weekly-pay gambit on multiple occasions with smaller outfits.

Do you see what just a little negotiating can do?

So why do people fail to negotiate? There are ten reasons:

1. They don't expect to negotiate.
2. They don't believe it is permitted.
3. They think if they try, there will be a penalty f or failing.
4. They fear rejection and embarrassment.
5. They simply don't know how.
6. They're intimidated.
7. They feel lucky to rate any pay at all.
8. They don't know the going rates for their labor and experience.
9. They're lazy, and it seems easier to just go with the flow.
10. They have no other offers.

You need to go into any meeting or interview with a negotiation plan. Expect to have a little back-and-forth, to hear offers and to make counteroffers. It is normal.

Also, outline the amount that is *ideal*, the amount that is *very good*, the amounts that are *minimally acceptable* and *unacceptable*, and *your walkaway amount*.

An ideal amount may be 20–50 percent above the top of the known range for your services, experience level, and educational attainment. You have learned, for example that your target job pays at most $80,000. If you get that figure to $96,000 and up, you're in ideal territory.

Why would they pay such a premium? Several reasons come to mind.

For one thing, the hole in their staff that they're trying to fill is costing their company money, far more than the premium they'll be paying you. They may be tired of searching for suitable candidates. You could be the best one, or the only one, to apply. You could do a really good sales job on them.

If you get them to $88,000, which is 10 percent above the range, then this could be considered *very good*.

If your goal is to earn far more than you're worth, $80,000 may be *unacceptable*. Besides, you may be able to rate that at several places, some of which offer better perks and atmospheres.

You could consider $70,000 as your *walkaway* offer. This is so low that you may not counter it with an offer of your own.

Knowing these pay levels and your preferences before you meet will give you guidance. It will also give you some self-confidence. You'll come across as a person that knows himself or herself, and this suggests that you are a person of principles and integrity.

So expect to negotiate, and plan for it.

Even at venues where they explicitly say, "There will be no negotiation"—and they are rare—you should treat that declaration as an attempt to negotiate on their part.

I heard this a little while ago, and I had to laugh, considering I teach negotiation. To me this is about as foolish as the wording at the top of a rental agreement that says, "Standard Lease." There are a zillion variations of that "standard" lease, did you know that? It's true; any lawyer can confirm this.

Why would they say "standard" when that form is anything but? They print it precisely to keep you from trying to negotiate with them. If they get you to abandon all hope of bargaining for something better, they've created a nifty shortcut to getting everything they demand, correct?

What a great ploy that is, when it works. And it works a lot.

Don't fall for it.

And don't worry. If you try to negotiate and they're utterly inflexible, not budging even a slight bit, then you can always accept what they offered, if you must. Seldom will they penalize you for trying to improve your lot.

And what if they do? Do you really want to work for such folks, who won't give an inch? What will happen after you join their team? Will they refuse to allow you to see a doctor during business hours if that is the only available appointment time?

Ultrastrict authoritarians are not pleasant employers. If you seek that, then join the military. But even here enlightened officers will know when to cut their troops a little slack.

Indeed the tenor of negotiations with a prospective employer will tell you a lot about them. Do they seem reasonable, even as they approve certain requests but decline others?

Employment is always about humanity, because we're offering our services. Slavery was abolished long ago. Employers need to keep relations positive throughout the onboarding process. If they don't and you do hire on, residual bitterness can fester. This can lead you to walking out soon after you came aboard, and this will be costly to the hirer.

There shouldn't be a penalty for trying to negotiate.

There's another thing to consider. Most companies exist to earn a profit. They want to recoup their costs and add something onto that figure. That is a *profit*. Thus companies expect to be paid more than they're worth, and the best companies want big earnings. This means they get a huge return on capital. *They are paid far more than they're worth.*

You are seeking exactly the same thing. Being in the business of *you*, you have it as your goal is to earn what you need and then some.

They need a profit, and so do you. So how can they find their own profit seeking as acceptable while deploring yours? Many will do this, but it is not consistent, and under scrutiny it comes across as utterly irrational.

As I noted before, a lot of people fail to negotiate their pay because they fear rejection and embarrassment. Don't be one of them.

First of all, not getting a job offer or the job itself is not a rejection of *you* as a person. You are not your labor. Your labor is one of many things that you produce. It is a product of you. It issues from you. But it isn't the whole of you. No employer purchases the whole of you. Again, that would entail slavery.

But let's say you feel rejection. You need *more* of it, not less, if you want to earn far more than you're worth.

I was speaking to a career coach whose story stands for this point. She was unemployed and tired of doing jobs she felt were beneath her. So she applied to more than 1,000 jobs, snared several interviews, and got more than a dozen offers. Some were well above $100,000 per year, and she took one on the East Coast.

By purposely exposing herself to a thousand-plus rejections, she learned that rejection gets easier and easier to take. And it isn't personal at all. It's all about business.

Her experience echoes what I teach in my book *The Law of Large Numbers: How to Make Success Inevitable.* Do enough of anything, and you'll improve. Do more than that, and you'll succeed. Exceed even that amount of activity, and you'll become a legend.

In a job negotiation, nothing is as powerful as having a competing offer. This is what a Law of Large Numbers employment campaign will give you. The reason to reach out to so many potential hirers is to make them compete for your services. When they're competing, they're negotiating. When they aren't, they're dictating. That's *dictating*, as in dictator, master, ruler, conqueror, and slave owner.

Frederick Douglass, the freed slave turned statesman, said it well: "Power gives up nothing without a struggle." When you, as a job candidate, have alternatives, and you make this fact known, you'll make suitors struggle to snare you. The law of supply and demand suddenly favors you and not the employer. You are in scarce supply, which means your price goes up.

"I should point out that while I'm most interested in this position, I do have some offers standing by. So I'd like to arrange something that will work well for both of us, OK?"

This sort of statement says many powerful things. You're in competition, Mr. or Ms. Employer. Time is of the essence. If we don't come to terms, I'll accept one of my other offers.

It is so important to have two or more offers that I would make this your primary goal. Other offers give you what experienced negotiators refer to as a BATNA. This is the *best alternative to a negotiated agreement*. You need to have a BATNA at all times to be an effective, confident negotiator. This means you have choices. You can entertain someone's offer without being compelled to grab it.

Back to the car example, if your existing ride has finally gone 100 percent kaput, and it won't start, you *must* get a new car. Therefore you'll pay a premium, because if you don't, you'll be walking or taking public transportation. But as long as your car is operational, you can still drive that, so you have a BATNA.

Multiple job offers are the best BATNAs because they say you are in demand. Everyone wants to hire a winner. It is the bandwagon effect. By being widely sought after, you assuage the concern that this particular employer will be taking a risk in making you an offer or in paying you a premium wage.

Remember: Ask and you will receive. Ask for more, and you'll receive more, both in offers and in pay!

Never Believe Money Is Scarce!

I follow about five major-league baseball teams. One of them is the Los Angeles Dodgers. This club has suffered through several owners since the longtime stewardship of the O'Malley family. A few years ago, they were purchased by Guggenheim Partners, a major investment company. For all intents and purposes, the Dodgers have very deep pockets. They can purchase the contracts of the best ballplayers in the game if they want to. But they don't, which puzzles observers like me. Sure, the owners are businesspeople, but making your team a world champion is good for business, even if it costs a pretty penny.

Even more of a mystery is how the fans make excuses for the owners. Again, the bosses can afford anyone they want. If they need a great pitcher, they can have him in a Dodger uniform in no time.

The fans forget this. Indeed they keep writing to the *Los Angeles Times* to the effect that "we can't have everything." But we can!

There is almost a hardwired belief that money is scarce, that we have to accept less than the best. I shouldn't be that surprised, because most folks bring the same scarcity thinking to their jobs and their careers. They act on the assumption that money is always in short supply. Companies can't afford to pay them a great wage because of this lack of funding.

In most cases, this is just plain wrong. It is what the late Zig Ziglar called "stinkin' thinkin.'" (Please see my book *Stinkin' Thinkin': 37 Mental Mistakes, False Beliefs, and Superstitions That Can Ruin Your Career and Your Life*.) It is a limiting way to view life, a fundamentally false and flawed perspective.

There is plenty of money. There is no shortage whatsoever. If your company wanted to double your pay in the blink of an eye, it could do just that. If there was a shortage of cash, the firm could borrow. Both banks and nontraditional lenders are lining up to rent funds to companies. Some of these sources are my consulting clients, so I know this firsthand.

Most folks have a poverty consciousness instead of a prosperity consciousness. They think poor instead of thinking rich. As Steve Jobs, cofounder of Apple, said, these folks need to "think different," even if that phrase isn't grammatical.

Speaking of Apple, it is presently sitting on a cash hoard of about $72 billion. Smart as this Silicon Valley company's managers are, they don't know what to do with these profits! Believe me, if they wanted to hire you or me, they could afford our wages or fees many times over.

Our job is *to get them to want to pay us bigger money*. And I have a surprise for you. *It is in their interest to do so.*

Better-paid people are happier. They're more stable, more productive, healthier, and more reliable.

I've seen an interesting correlation over the course of my career. Companies that have paid me hundreds of dollars have made thousands; those that have paid me hundreds of thousands have made millions!

Indeed *the more they pay me, the more they earn from my labor and brainpower.*

I mentioned a few reasons a second ago. The more I make, the more productive I am. It's like stepping up to the plate in an important game with the bases loaded. When I am counted on to deliver the big hit, I deliver.

Something else is also in play here. When companies and others pay us bigger bucks, they have more invested in us as players, and they want us to be productive. They give us more support. They don't want us to fail. If we do, it reflects badly on them. That dings their careers, which means they lose pay, perks, and privileges, and they don't want to have that experience.

Thus higher pay becomes a self-fulfilling prophesy. With a greater outlay of pay, employers expect a larger payback, and this expectation induces them to do what they can to assure such an outcome.

Let me give you a concrete example from my experience. I write books and record audio and video programs. Sometimes I publish under my own imprints, but often I negotiate with other publishers to bring my products to market. Authors are typically paid advance monies against royalties from sales. These advances give authors a small return on their investment of time and expertise.

Publishers that pay advances want to recover their investments. Therefore they'll usually promote the books they acquire fairly vigorously to avoid taking losses. When they promote, they succeed. If they fail to promote, they don't recoup advance monies or profit.

Many publishers refuse to offer advances. They mistakenly think having less invested in a product will provide them a greater profit margin and therefore greater profits. This is an illusion, because these authors are less likely to tell the world they have the products for sale.

When you're paid more, it's good for everyone!

This fact is truly counterintuitive.

Let's look at it from the consumers' perspective. How do they win if your wages are higher? Won't your elevated earnings result in higher prices for them?

Not necessarily, but even so, let's assume bigger wages translate into bigger prices. There are some benefits in paying more for things. In the first place, you create stability in the firm that is selling the item. With better wages, they retain employees, who are the same people that will provide you with customer service. Instead of having to adapt to one new face or voice after another, you'll become known to people. They can serve you better, because they know you, and you them.

Those that receive higher wages pay more in taxes. You'll drive on better paved roads and enjoy better government services because of their higher pay. They'll be less likely to require public support for food stamps, health care, and subsidized housing. They may be able to buy homes instead of renting. Home ownership is linked with community stability, lower crime, and higher real estate values.

This is really counterintuitive: when you pay more for a product or service, you hold it in higher regard. You feel better about it and take better care of it. In a word, you respect it more than you would if you thought it was cheap.

But those high prices aren't likely to stay high. Where profits grow, competitors go! Competition results in lower prices and better quality as more providers enter a market.

Your salary is someone else's living. With more income, you'll support more people, creating a multiplier effect, which brings a booming economy to more and more people.

In most countries where we find ultralow wages, we also find massive poverty. Advanced nations don't compete on price. They compete on added value.

And so should you when you sell your labor.

There's a book I hope you'll read called *Drive*. In it, author Daniel Pink says, "Higher wages could actually reduce a company's costs."

So *please don't think for a minute that you're taking advantage of anyone by being paid more.* Companies can pay and they should. It's good for you, and it's good for them, even if they bellyache about it.

Let me add a case study for you to consider in support of this concept.

I was looking to reduce employee turnover in companies that had inside sales units. I conducted a seminar across the country on the topic. How rampant was the turnover?

A major metropolitan newspaper has 300 people on the phones. They keep the average employee for only 3 months. This means they have to recruit, hire, train, and pay 1,200 people per year to keep the phones staffed. It takes a huge infrastructure to do this, many more employees on top of the 1,200 to keep this churning process going.

I calculated the out-of-pocket cost of this turnover to be in the millions of dollars. Here's the upshot. I determined that the paper could *double* the pay of its inside sellers and still save money by reducing the turnover.

By *not* paying you far more than you're currently earning, they're probably losing money. You're less motivated, less focused, and less likely to last. It's a lose-lose deal, the worst kind anyone can negotiate.

I'm here to tell say you can do a lot better.

Mastering the Performance Appraisal

There are a few arguments we have for getting better than average pay. One of them is that we hold the promise of great future performance. The other is that we have recently performed up to or beyond expectations.

The question of performance, of how we have done, is a matter of measuring sticks. By what standards can we say, "I'm a great achiever"?

Ideally, we would base this argument on a set of criteria established at the beginning of a performance period.

For example, it's the Christmas season. During this time nonretailers do a lot of planning for the next year, and it's natural to do performance reviews pertinent to the current year.

If you had specific projects that you needed to deliver, and deliver them you did, then a performance review can be pretty straightforward. It might even be enjoyable. "You said, 'Jump this high,' and I did it!" you can bellow.

But if the criteria for success have not been laid out in advance, which is typical of many smaller or family-run firms, then you're potentially shooting from the hip. This can feel uncomfortable and put you at a disadvantage.

"I did everything you asked me to do" is no doubt an accomplishment, but it is better to point to specific established objectives that you delivered.

MBO

This brings me to a topic that is very important in performance appraisals: *management by objectives*, also called MBO.

This is not a new concept. It has been around for several decades. It is actually a process by which employee performance is governed and made productive.

MBO sets forth a companywide goal known as the *prime objective*. This can be a numerical target. For example, a firm may want to grow its revenues by 20 percent.

You're in the sales department, which has a direct impact on revenues. Your sales quota may be increased by 20 percent or even by 30 percent, so if you or colleagues come up short, the company will still be on track to achieve its prime objective.

So far, so good, but how, specifically, are you going to reach this goal? Your specific action plan will light the path for you.

You may be given an objective to contact 40 percent more prospects than you're used to doing. The idea is that you'll achieve 30 percent more sales by reaching more people with your message.

Well, you already thought you were busy, so how are you going to find the time to contact 40 percent more people? This is one point where objectives are negotiated. Savvy managers will ask reps in your position what they can do to free up your time, to make you more efficient and effective.

You might suggest relieving you of a few accounts that seem to be consuming way too much of your time and attention. If they can be handed over to an assistant or to customer support, you'll be liberated, and even enthused.

It is incredibly important to be an activist in setting your performance objectives. Again, these are often negotiated.

So, using the example I just offered, you might believe 40 percent more contacts are impossible to make in the time allotted to you, no matter how many customers you unload to someone else. You need to point this out! If you remain silent, you're tacitly endorsing the idea that you'll easily make the adjustment. If this isn't true, you'll set yourself up for an incredible amount of stress and even failure.

It is also important, to the extent possible, to discuss the following question: "If I do achieve these numbers, what is in it for me?"

Will you see a 20 percent hike in pay, or a 10 percent bonus?

Equally important is this question: "If I substantially exceed target performance, raising my sales by 50 percent or more, what rewards can we agree that I'll see?"

Typically, MBO systems will provide answers. They'll define various levels of achievement. These could include: *substantially below target, below target, on target, above target,* and *substantially above target.* Occasionally MBO systems will have a superstar category, which is *exceeds all expectations.*

These distinctions in performance will pertain to each individual objective that you set. When all of your objectives are taken into account—and you might have had several at once—you'll be given one of these labels. You'll know where you stand; so will your managers, and so will their managers.

Another aspect of MBO is that objectives are often interlocking. In effect, your manager cannot earn substantially above target scores for his or her performance if your and his other reports are all below target or worse.

This alignment of purposes, goals, methods, and measures submits all participants in a firm to the same disciplines as well as opportunities for recognition. Nobody is left behind when it comes to receiving a holiday bonus, providing they have met their targets.

At this time, your company may not have MBO as a general management tool. But this shouldn't stop you from negotiating your own, personal MBO program with your boss!

You should start a dialogue at once. "I'd like to sit down with you, boss, and discuss my objectives and goals for the next thirty days. Would that be OK?"

Then you can go through a list of your duties. Focus on the priorities for getting things done, from the boss's viewpoint.

Various questions can ferret out your prime objective or objectives:

"If we were to accomplish the single most important item on this list, what would it be?"

"If we had to jettison anything, or deemphasize its importance, what would that be?"

By an act of Congress, the United States Navy, along with other branches of the federal civil service, was required to introduce an incentive pay plan for its employees. This was a massive program. I was recruited to be an instructor, and, along with others, trained 18,000 senior-level Navy administrators in MBO.

According to the admiral who oversaw this initiative, we delivered a hugely successful program on time and on target. We met all of our objectives!

I was assigned to the Naval Research Laboratory in Washington. My job was to train senior scientists, and it was quite a challenge.

One of their concerns was setting objectives for achievement in a field where failure is success. Scientists need to run experiments. Not all experiments yield successful results, but they could be successful experiments anyway.

We might be seeking a stealth coating for submarines. Various chemicals will be combined. Many won't produce the desired breakthrough, but they are still valuable, because they tell us what *not* to try in the future. They rule out certain compounds.

I won't go into details here, but we found a way of measuring success and helping the scientists to achieve using the MBO process.

The learning point is this: no matter what job you do, setting objectives with your boss will help you to prove your worth and to qualify for substantially above target earnings!

Don't Settle for the First Offer

Here is another important negotiation concept:

Seldom is the first offer made to you the best offer that party can make.

They say they'll pay you a salary of $60,000. What tells us that is all the money they have, can afford, or are willing to pay?

An assumption does. We assume: *The first offer is the best offer.*

As with every assumption, it needs to be put to the test.

"Gee, thank you, but I'm looking for more," you say and then shut up.

The ball is in their court. What will they say? "OK, you can leave. Goodbye"?

That's doubtful. If they like you and have gotten to the point that they make an offer, then they're not going to toss you away, at least not like that.

They might reply, "How much are you looking for?"

Then it's up to you to pick a number.

If you go with 10 percent you're at $66,000. A 20 percent uptick will put you at $72,000.

They'll do one of several things. They might claim to not have the authority to bump your offer. They could use a third-party excuse: "I'll have to speak to my boss about that."

Or they could counteroffer: "$72K is way above our range for this job, but I may be able to get this to $65K or to $66K."

Then you're in business!

With a solid and improved offer, you can use this technique, popularized by guru Roger Dawson:

"Well, I'd love to accept. Let's see, I'm at 72 and you're at 66. That's a difference of only six thousand. I'll split the difference with you, making it 69, fair enough?"

Normally I don't believe in splitting the difference. But in this case, they've already come up to a decent level, so if you split the difference at that point, you'll seem generous. But the key is to stick to your original, highest figure, while splitting *their highest figure*, which is 66, not 60!

If they stall, don't be afraid to say, "I'd really like to get started. Let's plan to speak again tomorrow, OK?"

Or you can make them a little paranoid that they'll lose you: "I'd really like to start here, but I am looking at some higher offers. So please let me know what you can do. Let's speak again tomorrow, OK?"

Here I've thrown in a few persuasive devices that you'll want to use. Note what I do at the ends of certain points.

I'll state my preference and then tie it down. "Let's plan to speak tomorrow," I said, and concluded with "OK?"

That *OK* is designed to get a commitment.

In an earlier example, I did the same thing with a different ending.

I said, "I'll split the difference with you, making it sixty-nine, fair enough?"

Expect to have some give-and-take. This is customary.

Some people say in a successful negotiation nobody gets everything they want. We give up more than we expected, or we get less than we hoped, but so does the other person. What we end up with is a livable agreement.

Are there employers that will state an initial figure and not budge from that? Yes, there are. They are called *positional negotiators*, according to Harvard researchers. These employers will say, "We'll give you $60K and that's our best offer." You want to respond with this question: "May I asked how you arrived at $60K?"

They could reply, "That's the market value for this job."

"According to what sources?" you could press.

If they come up empty, you can ask, "If I can show you that $70K is closer to market value, will you pay that?"

Now you've put them in a box. They want to pay $60K; who doesn't? Maybe they'll find someone to accept $60K, but is that person known to them now? How much will they invest to recruit that individual? Typically recruiting can cost $6K to $10K for a position.

Are they willing to sink that money into searching for another acceptable candidate?

What does it cost that company to have this position remain open? It has to cost more than your salary, perhaps three to ten times more, depending on their profit margins. What's cheaper? To keep losing money with that vacancy or pay you slightly more and get back on track now?

This isn't rocket science. Many job seekers are reluctant to discuss the economic value they are providing through their labor. It is as if they believe they have to have a doctorate to earn the right.

That's wrong. Let me give you analogy.

Let's say you're leasing an apartment or house. You've been a good tenant. But the landlord tells you that there will be a $300 rent increase, effective when the lease ends.

That amounts to $3,600 per year, which is a tidy sum. If your rent is at $2,400 now, this means the landlord will lose money if he or she cannot find a replacement lessee within 6 weeks of your departure.

You can explain that point and agree to renew for another year at the current rate: $2,400. Or you can agree to a $100 increase. It's up to you.

The point is that time passes, and the passage of time is *costly* to the person on the other side of the bargaining table. Signal to them that you understand this concept.

Believe me, they know it as well. They don't want to show it, but they'll have to accede to its logic if you point it out to them.

Employers are not stupid, but they'll willingly seem that way if it will save them money. You must appeal to their self-interest, and the best way to do this is with a discussion of economic realities.

Let me add one more thing, and this is crucial. The labor market can shift dramatically, making your labor worth far more than it was mere months beforehand.

I teach negotiation at UC Berkeley and UCLA, the number-one and number-two ranked public universities in the United States. Students in my seminars are working people with a keen sensitivity to the marketplace.

For the last two years, my attendees in San Francisco have acted in an unusually self-confident manner in role-plays dealing with employment negotiations. This is a dramatic change. Before that time, for at least four or five years, they were cowed by the recession.

I asked them if the tide had turned. I asked, "Are jobs easier to get, and are wages rising?" To a person, say replied, "Yes!"

At long last, my Los Angeles participants agree.

Labor is in demand. This means it may be the most promising time to get paid far more than you're worth!

Ask for more, and you'll get more. Pit one employer against another. Hop from post to post. Apply for positions in different sections of your current company. Ride the tide!

What if you're in a labor backwater, where wages are relatively depressed?

The techniques I'm giving you will still work. But you may want to move where market favors *you*!

How to Sell Yourself

I probably don't have to tell you about Sir Richard Branson. He is a British entrepreneur who founded all things Virgin: Virgin Records, Virgin Airways, and so on.

He was quoted as saying, "If you find an opportunity, seize it. Don't concern yourself about whether you are capable of achieving it. If it is a job, you'll learn how to do it after you have accepted the post."

This is utterly backwards, isn't it?

But he is correct. He has to be. After all, he is a billionaire.

Most opportunities don't simply happen. They're created, and we are the ones that need to generate them.

Simply put, we need to sell ourselves into opportunities that can deliver above-average incomes and lifestyles.

To sell ourselves, we need selling skills. I am the best-selling author of the book, *Selling Skills for the Non-salesperson*, and I have personally trained and coached thousands of nonsellers, so I feel uniquely equipped to summarize what you need to do and the abilities you need to have.

The first thing is to adopt a certain mind-set. You need to change your outlook about selling. Most people hate it. They don't like glad-handing. The stereotype of the salesperson as a do-anything and say-anything person without a soul is very unattractive.

Parenthetically, what's really interesting is that among nontechnical jobs, developed economies such as ours need more salespeople than just about any other kind of worker.

There is a good reason. Selling, as an activity, is crucial to getting things done. Selling boils down to developing an offer and presenting it to a person in a position to buy.

If you're job hunting, your offer is your labor, and you want someone to buy it, plain and simple.

Even you are like me, where you don't exactly become an employee, but you are developing more of a partnership, you're still selling. I am constantly developing intellectual properties. These are seminars and training programs, books, videos, audios, and articles. Every one of them requires distribution. Books, audios, and videos need publishers. Courses need universities and other venues where they'll be staged. In every case, I'm reaching out to them, as well as to agents who can represent my projects.

In a way, selling is never-ending, even for people who don't think they sell. These folks—and you could be one of them—are actually being outsold by others who are better at this function.

What prevents us from selling effectively, besides our negative stereotypes? Most people suffer from shyness. According to researcher Philip Zimbardo of Stanford, 80 percent of us are shy in one situation or another.

For many, this translates into stage fright. Public speaking is a nightmare scenario. Others are phone-shy. They're afraid to pick up the phone.

Other people don't mind telephoning but are paralyzed by the idea of having a one-on-one job interview.

There are a few good ways to overcome any phobia. One is systematic desensitization. Purposely do what which scares you. Not once. Do it a lot!

For instance, I recommend using the phone to secure job interviews. Let's say you have answered an ad with a cover letter and a résumé. Typically, these by themselves will put you on the same level as hundreds if not thousands of other job seekers. But if you pick up the phone and call the employer, referring to your résumé and cover letter, you'll put yourself into very rare company. You'll stand out from the crowd.

Even if your phone approach is amateurish or terribly flawed or makes you cringe in shame and embarrassment, it will be better than not calling. Why?

You'll be saying several things with your outreach attempt. In the first place, you're saying you really want this job—enough to do something extra to earn it. Think about that for a second. You're willing to go the extra mile.

From a practical standpoint, you'll also be persuading people to dig your paperwork out of a pile of competing applications. It will be a flag that your candidacy should be given special consideration.

Moreover, a call is a communication. Communication skill is something required by more and more jobs, so you'll be proving your merit in this department.

Above all, if the position you're seeking has anything to do with persuasion, selling, assertiveness, or leadership, your attempt will speak well for your possession of these attributes.

You might be the only person who calls! That will put you into the company of one. In what other way could you so quickly obtain a competitive advantage over an avalanche of other applicants?

A phone call can also open you to a world of unadvertised opportunities, what is sometimes called the hidden job market.

As with an iceberg, most job opportunities are not visible to the average job seeker, who relies only on posted listings on the Internet and at employment agencies. You won't find these hidden opportunities unless you have a personal connection to the employer. When you're on the phone, having a meaningful conversation, you can ask, "What other jobs are you aware of in the company that I should learn about? Is there anyone else I should acquaint myself with?"

The savvy person makes more opportunities than he or she is given. When you're selling yourself, this is what you're doing—you're multiplying opportunities.

Let's get down to specifics. What does an effective outreach call sound like?

Like many sales talks, it has four parts: an *opener*, a *description*, a *close*, and a *confirmation*.

"Hello, my name is Gary Goodman, and I just applied for your customer-service position. I thought you might like to put a voice to my name and flag my application, if you'd be so kind."

This is a very powerful beginning. It gets to the point. It states a benefit: the hirer can hear my voice, which is a job-related strength. And I have actually asked for special consideration. I have more or less asked the person to flag my application, to take special notice of it. The line I have provided is a microsale in itself.

The *opener* is my name and my saying I applied. This is a justification for my phone approach.

The *description* is where I provide benefits, referring to hearing my voice.

The *close* is asking for some action, in this case flagging the application.

And I almost have a *confirmation*, which is where we restate what we've agreed to. "If you'd be so kind" is such a restatement. If the person says, "OK, I'll make a note" or "I'll pass this along" or "Thank you for calling," it will signal success.

Even if they say they don't accept calls, it's too late! You did call, and you stated your business and your intention.

How can they *not* be influenced by this contact as they consider the applications they have received?

You'll stand out even if they say you won't stand out.

By the way, if the person that takes your call is rude, that doesn't speak well of the company. It is especially inauspicious if it is a person you'll be reporting to. But there is another implication. You might want to speak to someone else if you're seeking a better reception or if that particular job or company is important to you.

This is how a salesperson would interpret a given person's rudeness: it is just one person's reaction. You may be reaching out to a firm with a thousand employees. Why would you allow yourself to be derailed by someone who is in a bad mood and may not be critical to the hiring decision?

Companies have several doors. One of them was guarded by a troll. Try another door!

There are a few sales lessons here to consider.

One pertains to the idea of rejection. You're selling yourself, so it feels like a personal rejection if they're saying no to you as an applicant. This can sting, if you let it.

You need to tell yourself it isn't personal. In most cases, not getting what we want from a person has more to do with their mood and their personal agenda at the moment than it has to do with us.

Another thing to remember is the Law of Large Numbers. As I've already pointed out, if you do enough of anything, you'll get good at it and succeed. Do more than that, and you'll prosper. Exceed even that amount of exertion, and you'll become a legend.

If we look at rejection, this idea would have us knowingly and deliberately attempt to be rejected a lot. As we've had the experience of hearing no and even being treated rudely, we become inured to it. We develop a thick skin. Each subsequent sting would become less painful until we got to a point where we wouldn't care at all.

What would be the advantage in all of this suffering? We would inevitably find acceptance at least some of the time.

When I was a sales manager at Time-Life, one of my better salesmen went on job interviews at nearby firms. He had no intention of leaving Time-Life. He was curious. He wanted to know how they paid their sellers, what the working hours were, and how much their reps were earning. He'd report his findings to me, and we'd have some laughs. We'd also get a sense of how good our company really was.

In almost every case, those that interviewed him offered him a job on the spot. He was almost universally sought after, for a few reasons. For one thing, he got really good at doing interviews, because he got so much practice. And because he had an experimental attitude and was willing to be rejected, he gave off the vibration that he didn't really need any specific job. All of which made him more desirable.

When you're selling yourself, you need to see the big picture. There are tons of jobs out there. You wouldn't have enough time in a hundred lifetimes to interview for all of the opportunities. The company you are contacting is lucky to be in your presence. It actually has a chance to snare your skills.

Don't become arrogant about this. Simply be aware that positions abound. This is the hard fact that my employee knew. He was in demand.

By applying the Law of Large Numbers to interviewing, he discovered this bedrock truth. I want you to enjoy the benefits of believing as he did.

You can take a page from his book and schedule ceaseless interviews while you're employed elsewhere, or even as an unemployed person. Imagine you don't need any particular offer. Adopt an experimental attitude.

If you feel you blew it in one meeting, comfort yourself. There will be another and another after that.

This is a point that I make in my Best Practices in Negotiation seminars and book: negotiators are afraid of mistakes. Why? They assign too much importance to any particular bargain that they're making at the time. It's like believing your next meal will be your last. It's simply untrue. There will be another. It is OK to leave a few crumbs on the plate.

I should point out that while my employee was doing his job-seeking experiment, he was having a blast. This is what happens when you're playing a game. Yes, it's fun to win, but playing is the object of the exercise.

When it's nice and fun to win, but not exceedingly important or crucial to do so, you have the right attitude. This is the way professional job seekers feel about their task. You can't win them all, though you may try. Like baseball players, you may still be a pro and get a hit only twice in ten at-bats. You're Hall of Fame material when you can hit safely three out of ten times on average.

Who is wired to accept or to actively seek ten possible rejections, only to be favored with positive outcomes three of those times?

Salespeople and athletes are, and you need to be as well if you want to find the type of job that will pay you more than you're worth.

Make Them Pay You in Perks!

I'm keenly interested in those annual surveys reported in the business press. They say that when it comes to job satisfaction, money doesn't come in first place. It's typically in third place or thereabouts.

I scratch my head when I see such surveys. I think they're inherently invalid, because a lot of people don't want to seem money-hungry. At the same time, they cannot deny its importance, so they bury it further down the list than it rightfully belongs.

Still, this sort of survey does raise a question that is pertinent to our discussion. Apart from money, what are some other ways you can get paid far more than you're worth? Money is simply one way to be paid. There are many others, including what I call *money equivalents*.

There are lots of people that don't earn much money from their work, but they're paid plenty overall. How can that happen?

For one thing, you can choose an employer or an industry that provides a major perk. Let's say you work for an airline. You can expect to get huge discounts on airfares; sometimes you'll only be asked to pay the taxes on your itinerary. What can this benefit add up to?

I know someone that worked for a carrier in customer service. She traveled to faraway places at least twice a year. If she had paid for the airfare, it would have set easily her back $10,000–15,000.

Let me be even more specific. When an ordinary person buys an airline ticket, she is paying for it in after-tax dollars. If she is flying for pleasure, she cannot get a tax write-off, so every dollar she pays to an airline is a net dollar, one that she got after she paid taxes on the money. Pleasure is expensive if you cannot tie it to business.

Why Incorporate?

Speaking of which, if you incorporate, so that you're Josie Jones, Inc. instead of just Josie Jones the worker, there are lots of advantages. You can access a number of business deductions that would not be permitted for an individual. The United States tax code gives special treatment given to businesses. Government policy provides tax perks because it wants people to form new enterprises.

When a company pays your earnings to Josie Jones, Inc. it is typically paying you 100 percent of your gross earnings. It is up to you, and your accountant, to set aside a certain amount for payroll taxes if you intend to take a salary. You also have to pay your own Social Security taxes. But these aren't burdens when you evaluate the advantages of having 100 percent of your funds with which to operate.

You can also deduct the computers and other electronics that you'd buy as an individual as legitimate business expenses. A portion of your home that is used primarily or exclusively for business purposes can also be expensed. Ditto for your Internet connections, pens, pencils, writing tablets, and postage. Work-related car expenses, gasoline, and insurance can also receive favored tax treatment.

Having a separate corporation will bring down your taxable income. In some years, this may mean you'll break even or show an operating loss. By expensing ordinary and necessary items, you'll get more complete use of your money, which is the same thing as earning far more money than you're earning now.

Several states, including Nevada and Delaware, have no corporate income tax, so if you incorporate in them, you won't face double taxation as both an individual and as a company.

Typically the cost to incorporate is several hundred dollars, so it's not as expensive as you might think. Nor do you need a lot of employees. You can serve as the president, secretary, and treasurer all rolled into one. You'll still need to pay federal taxes, but these can be legally minimized, which is the standard practice of most for-profit enterprises.

Speaking of which, you could incorporate as a nonprofit organization, if the purpose of your entity pursues not-for-profit objectives. If you are really a teacher or a trainer, you could open a school. While this may seem out of reach for most people, most nonprofits are exceedingly modest, operating on paper-thin budgets.

One primary benefit of nonprofits is that they are typically exempt from having to pay either federal or state income taxes. This means they get to use 100 percent of every dollar that comes in. Incorporating multiplies the value of each dollar you receive. This could be the equivalent of giving yourself a 50–100 percent raise in pay overnight.

When you're in your own business, you can bargain for your pay and perks, and you can set up similar compensation structures. Being incorporated might help you in this regard.

What other perks can a company can give you? Some are basic. One is food. I've consulted for a number of companies that have subsidized cafeterias. If you eat at work, you can save a bundle and add variety to your diet.

Other organizations offer subsidized housing. Some professors at Pepperdine University in Malibu, California, enjoy multimillion dollar ocean views for a fraction of the price this housing would cost on the open market.

This could be a perk worth up to $5,000 or $10,000 per month in after-tax earnings. We're talking about $60,000 to $120,000 of money-equivalent income each year.

Where you work is your choice. Why would you choose to work at a place that has zero perks?

Time: Your Most Precious Resource

Let's talk about the one thing that is more precious to us than anything else, whether we realize it or not. It is our *time*. There is only so much of it. How much we trade for a certain amount of income is also a major decision.

Let's say a given company is willing to pay you $75,000 per year. That may be an attractive figure to you. What if they'll allow you to work your own hours, and you can do a meritorious job by putting in only 20–25 hours per week? How much are you earning? Is it still $75,000?

From one perspective, you are making twice that amount, because the job is only asking you for a part-time commitment. Theoretically, you could do two of those jobs simultaneously and earn $150,000.

You might be wondering where can you find this kind of job.

Certainly you can find some in the sales field, where most managers are really looking at your results achieved rather than at the time you put on the clock. As long as you make your quota, qualify for your bonus, or measure up right on the current yardstick, you probably don't have to worry about watching the clock. (If you fall below a certain level of production, the time you invest will come into greater scrutiny.) So selling jobs often provide you with a lot of slack when it comes to your time investment. This is a big perk, which in itself can provide you with far more income than you'd expect.

But there are part-time jobs everywhere that are masquerading as full-time work. They say that forty or more hours are expected, but when you are on-site, you find that the reality is very different. People saunter in between 8:30 and 9:15. They leave anywhere from 4:00 to 4:45. Yet the employee manual says they have to be there from 8 to 5:30. What gives?

Official work rules call for one behavior, yet in fact another behavior is in place that follows an informal, unstated rule.

I recall working at a mutual fund company as a consultant. At one point I was told by one of the senior managers to whom I reported, "As long as you're in by

8:30 and you leave at 5:30, you'll be fine. You can take two-hour lunches and enjoy a relaxed work flow if you get your job done." So they were sticklers for punching in and out, but in the middle of the day, they were very laid-back. This meant I could get some of my outside work done on their dime, and still everyone was happy.

I'd say about three hours each day were mine to manage for personal purposes. So was I really working full-time?

I don't think so. Three out of eight is 37.5 percent of the working day. Technically, you could say I was working not half-time, but a little more: 62.5 percent of the day. Translate that into money, and I was earning a 37.5 percent premium on top of my consulting fees.

That, my friend, is being paid more than you're worth!

Even if you are on a company's payroll, how much time you must put in to earn a unit of pay is variable. Much of it is under your control. The less time and effort that is required of you, the more you are being paid.

Of course, there are other perks besides being able to manage your time. I've mentioned housing. Companies can also provide you with cars, which can be major perks.

When I graduated from college, I went to work for an upscale Beverly Hills auto-leasing company. It expected account executives like me to be well received by affluent clients, so we were provided with new cars to drive, along with car insurance. These perks are worth a lot, believe me. In current dollars, we're talking about $500 to $1,250 a month in extra nontaxable earnings.

When our cars racked up about 2,000 miles, we leased them to our customers at a slight discount, and we got even newer rides. We were never bored, I can tell you!

Let's reflect on this perk as well as harking back to airline discounts. In both cases, the costs to the employers were minimal. Even these days, with packed flights, airlines have some unsold seats, and the leasing company was still able to rent out the "drivers" they had given us staffers.

In other words, the income equivalent was very high to employees, but the expense to the companies was very low. This is really a win-win scenario. This is what you're looking to get for yourself.

Where you work is also potentially a major perk. I live on one of the Channel Islands in Southern California. Our backyard is a canal that leads to the Pacific Ocean. The view rivals that of Venice. This is what I look at as I make business calls and do my writing.

For me, not commuting for an hour or more in traffic to go to an office, while enjoying the beauty around me, are major perks. I have a million-dollar view. On a moment's notice, I can take a walk, go kayaking, or drive a few minutes to bodysurf at one of the best beaches in the world. I chose this for myself. Although very few of these benefits appear as money in the bank, they constitute much of my practical wealth.

Some time ago I had a conversation with my brother-in-law, who grew up in a noisy borough of New York City. "There were always sirens in the middle of the night," he remembered.

He decided to move to California's beautiful Monterey peninsula, specifically to Pebble Beach. He wasn't much of a golfer, but he reveled in the natural beauty and the whisper-quiet evenings.

"Gary, I'd rather live in a shack up here than in a palace in the middle of the city," he said with utter conviction.

I believe him. Living in a satisfying place, whatever that means to you, may be worth a fortune.

Let's say you have average skills, and you feel you're destined, at least in the short term, to work in an average job, with average pay for that job.

Why not do that job in paradise?

Paradise may be Nashville, Indiana, with its beautiful autumn leaves and local arts scene. It could be hot biscuits topped with local apple butter. It could be Hawaii, or downtown Los Angeles.

Work there!

We have a mobile work force. Move to a better place. I read once that if you move to paradise, paradise will find a way to support you. With telecommuting and the Internet, this is truer than ever.

A company may not give you exceptional money. Make them pay you in perks. If they won't pay for them, move to where you're happy so as to provide them for yourself.

Chapter 4

Mastering the Psychology of Getting Paid More

I was finishing my PhD and job hunting.

I went to the two major conventions scheduled during my last year in the doctoral program. One was in Phoenix, close to LA, where I lived. The other was in Washington, the nation's home office.

My budget was tight, but I had to go to these events to interview for the few college teaching jobs that were available in the United States.

One post seemed almost perfect. Located in rural Indiana, it was a decent liberal-arts university, the type that Mr. Chips could have found appealing. About an hour from Indianapolis and three and a half from Chicago, it was a livable location.

And that was about it as far as jobs for which I was qualified were concerned. One and only one chance was out there for me to do what I had been training for many years to do. That's pretty grim.

I hope you don't prepare yourself for such a sorry fate.

Let me make it worse, if I may. I was actually about to move across the country, leaving a metropolis with all of its excitement, sophistication, and, yes, restaurants, for less money than I made as a graduate student.

But it was expected of me. I was a star coming out of grad school. One of the best and brightest, I simply had to score the only pertinent tenure-track teaching job in my field.

I pulled out all of the stops to make this happen. I lobbied my professors to contact their friends at the targeted school. My department chair pushed for me. I even had profs in my corner who didn't like me very much but were persuaded by my argument that I would add to their prestige.

But there was a huge obstacle in the way. The fellow who was already at this school, teaching in the position I sought, had also applied. Up to that point he had been a temp, but now they made the job permanent. What had been a year-to-year gig was now tenure-track. This meant it could go on forever.

This sort of job security is rare. It makes a poorly paying post much more attractive for a certain kind of security-minded individual. Where else but academia can you find a forty-year sinecure?

So my rival was revved up to get it. He was also published in the field, which gave him an advantage. Worse, the students and faculty liked him, and apparently he liked them, or pretended to sufficiently. In a very real sense, he had been auditioning for the job for a long time.

By comparison, an outsider like me would have no chance. It would be like a lightweight knocking out the heavyweight champion of the world. Who was I kidding?

But this isn't how I felt. I thought destiny was in my corner. I convinced myself the hand of Providence would sweep away all opposition, including that pesky foe who had beaten me to the scene.

I applied, and the school flew me back twice to meet and greet. I was also asked to audition, to prepare a lecture that would be attended by the meek and the powerful—students, faculty, and administrators.

I left the campus on both occasions feeling more and more confident. When I got back to my graduate school, the University of Southern California, everybody wanted to know what I thought. Did I get it? Was the position mine?

A long silence ensued, and I was going nuts with anticipation, which turned to dread. I hadn't heard anything. Finally, after I phoned the provost, I was told that the job went to the other guy.

No one could believe it. They thought it was in the bag.

I refused to give up. I told them I was sorry I didn't get the nod, but that they should please keep me in mind if anything else opened up.

I continued to see myself teaching at that school. I dreamed about it. I was consumed by it. I simply had to win, and I refused to lose.

A few weeks passed, and the phone rang. The school asked me if I was still available, and I said, "Sure!"

The position was mine if I could finish my dissertation in time to meet my first classes at the end of August. It didn't leave me much time, but I was motivated. I finished, hitched the U-Haul trailer to my car, and made it to Indiana on time.

This is when things started to unravel.

Adrenalin, ego, guts, and boundless energy enabled me to snatch victory from the jaws of defeat. As the autumn chill filled the air and my eyes cleared, I started to feel I had won the battle. But I was now in for a long and bruising war.

They didn't create an additional position for me. They did appoint the other guy. I was defeated. He won. Reportedly he had become so battered by the process that once he was hired for the permanent post that he quit, accepting a position at a school in a neighboring state.

Of course, this turn of events is a tribute to my candidacy. Even though the other guy enjoyed all the advantages of incumbency, I rocked his professional world. I came so close to dislodging him that he couldn't live with that fact. The amateur wasn't knocked out in a humiliating way in an early round. I wasn't mopped up by the wily and highly favored title holder. I pushed the contest to the limit. There was no knockout. He won, probably by a split decision of the judges. He nosed me out on points, and probably not a whole lot of them. That was shameful to him, so he split.

But I didn't see, at least not right away, that his allies and champions would have it out for me. In his absence, they'd make sure that my stay at that school wasn't a pleasant one.

The chairman was newly appointed. He had changed from a person in my corner to a guy in my rival's corner. The new leader gave me four courses to prepare. I had maybe a month to finish my doctorate, which is writing a book. In that same time, I had to prep four semester-length classes.

In addition, I had to cocoach the debate team and run an honors conference, hosting luminaries from the entire country at a high-profile event. This was a back-breaking load, and even the most experienced professors would have found it intimidating.

Like practically every job candidate who finally obtains a position, I was exhausted by the time I arrived at the campus. I could have used a vacation. Instead I was being pushed beyond all reasonable limits.

I did pretty well, but not a perfect job, by my standards. But I read what was happening politically. I would never be granted tenure by my colleagues. There was no career at that place for me moving forward.

By November, I had made a decision to resign, only two months after my arrival. I fulfilled my contract, and taught until June.

I launched a successful and very lucrative seminar teaching business, which I have already described. Fortunately, this venture was fully functional and profitable by the time I loaded the local antiques I had acquired in the U-Haul for the return trip to California.

My story illustrates this fact, stated concisely by Sun Tzu in his famous treatise *The Art of War*:

"Victory with exhaustion means defeat in the battle to come."

I won the position, moving heaven and earth to do it. My irresistible force confronted the immovable object. I kept pushing. It cracked.

You can want something so badly that you change the course of mighty rivers and leap over buildings in a single bound, like Superman. In the process, you develop a stronger will. This ability to set forth an intention and to realize its fulfillment is worth many times the discomfort I experienced.

You should probably do this once, if only to confirm your belief that you can. But when the smoke clears from the battlefield, there will be a certain amount of destruction if your job candidacy has been contentious or acrimonious. You need to know this.

You know the adage, "Keep your powder dry." This means you need to preserve your ammunition. In the job hunt, this means your energy, your enthusiasm, and your positive attitude. If you are so war-weary by the time your hard-won job starts, you will be a victor, but not for long.

Here are some takeaways that I hope you'll take to heart.

Don't paint yourself into a corner by pursuing that one dream job to the exclusion of others. Keep your options open.

If you're in a field that only has one genuine job opportunity, that is a very poor field to be in. College teaching turned out this way for me.

To kick off the academic year, the president of that university gave a speech to the faculty. This took place in a beautiful, ivy-covered building, and it seemed to be an auspicious occasion. The speaker was well prepared, as you would expect, but his talk was unintentionally depressing. He said college enrollments were expected to decline in the ensuing years, and nothing could be done about it. Budgets would be strained; belts would be tightened.

I heard enough to conclude that I was probably in a very dismal industry: that of teaching college undergraduates. His talk also convinced me that he was not the person to lead us out of the impending abyss.

One job existed in a dying field, and I was destined to apply for it. What could be better?

You get the picture.

If an ill wind blows, change course quickly. This is another important lesson. I didn't apply its wisdom only at that university. Over the course of my career, I've been connected to a number of firms that came under siege for various reasons. One of these firms was racking up a surprising number of unsatisfied clients. As soon as a new one was put on the books, a different one defected. Simple math told me it wasn't sustainable.

Even more damning was the feeling in the air. The place felt stifling. Everyone knew there was something fundamentally wrong, but no one would speak about it. That feeling drained energy and stifled creativity.

Again, victory with exhaustion makes no sense.

One more point, if I may: People do not live by prestige alone. Having that tenure-track job was highly prestigious. Many were called, as the expression says, but only one was chosen. (Well, technically two, but you know that story.)

I was in exclusive company! You couldn't buy the degrees or college posts that I earned through sacrifice, study, and, yes, hard work and talent.

Let me share a story about status and prestige.

There was a fellow who cleaned up after the elephants at the circus. To many, his job was less than delightful.

But when he was asked, "Why don't you quit?" he replied: "What—leave *show business*?"

We know that winning the battle, but losing the war is foolhardy. Yet this is exactly the kind of thing we do when we pursue certain opportunities.

Remember, just because you can get the job doesn't mean you should take it. If the process leaves you feeling exhausted, or it creates enemies and collateral damage, it may not mean that you won after all.

Hitch Your Wagon to a Win-Win Company

There are three kinds of companies: those that will allow to you make significantly above-average money, those that might let it happen, and those that will not do so in any case.

These companies coincide with the three types of arrangements that we fashion as negotiators. These are win-win, win-lose, and lose-lose. I see this in my negotiations all the time.

Some people want the best for themselves, and they don't mind if others prosper too. In fact they expect it. They belong to the category of persons who see the world of human relations as one of reciprocity. Give-and-take, something for something—these are the agreements and relationships that they endorse. To them, if they hope to prosper, why wouldn't everyone else want the same?

Isn't that the way normal people think? It is, but there aren't that many normal people. I estimate that only 20 percent of the population believe or act as if reciprocity governs the planet.

A full 60 percent see life as a zero-sum game. If they win, someone has to lose. It's sweet and sour, good and bad. This view is based on scarcity: there isn't enough to go around. Someone has to draw the short straw. Of course, they don't want it to be them.

You could wonder about the origins of these personalities. Did some folks not get enough baby formula? Did all of their big brothers and sisters snatch the cookies before they got a bite?

I don't know, and it doesn't matter how these people came to be the way they are. They believe there is one loaf, and they want more than half.

The third type of person produces lose-lose outcomes. Their goal is to prevent others from winning. They're spoilers. They don't even mind losing themselves. Indeed they probably lose a lot and expect it. They just want to be sure that you do not win.

I knew a bitter college professor who was like this. He wouldn't prepare his lessons, because he was jealous of his students. He knew that they, with their family connections, were destined for a secure upper-middle-class life, whereas he was doomed to scraping by on the fringes of the lower middle class because he had chosen to teach.

Sure, he could have augmented his earnings by consulting or by teaching summer sessions, but he preferred to wallow in self-pity, bemoaning his fate. He couldn't see his own destructiveness.

This man took it upon himself to ruin the career of a fellow professor. Knowing the colleague had a drinking problem, the lose-lose fellow decided to disparage the other guy's credentials. At every meeting, he disparaged him: he was unprepared, had only an outdated master's degree instead of a doctorate, and so forth.

Within a year or two of this abuse, the vilified colleague died of an apparent heart attack.

Did his tormentor benefit? He did, by becoming chair of the department, but he would have gladly done anything to stymie the other guy. No direct benefit to him was needed to provoke his caustic behavior.

I'm detailing this case for you to make a point. Lose-lose types will simply not permit you to make lemonade out of lemons. They are filled with contempt. They aren't motivated by dangling a carrot in front of them. They want to keep others from reaching the treat.

In such companies and organizations, it is simply foolish to think that you're going to break the bank. By staying, you'll be settling for scraps, and it's likely you'll become an embittered no-win type yourself.

Get away as fast as you can. Hook up with win-win types.

Who are they and where are they? In my experience, entrepreneurial personalities are the best to partner with. I've found many of them heading up their own small businesses.

Others work in sales. They like goodies, as a rule, and they know that there's more where that came from. They're not invested in the false belief that our economy is built on scarcity.

I've walked into more than a few businesses as a consultant and as an employment applicant where a wonderful thing happened. When I was touring the site, someone took me aside and whispered, "There's a lot of money to be made here!"

Imagine that! People took the effort to say, "Hey, hope you brought a shovel, because there's gold in them there hills!"

In a couple of cases, they were absolutely right. One place quickly led to more than a million dollars in earnings.

There is a great scene in the movie *The Color of Money*, starring Paul Newman as a professional pool hustler and Tom Cruise as his protégé. They walk into a billiards den, and Newman challenges Cruise's instincts.

"You smell that?" Newman asks.

"What?" Cruise wonders.

"Money," Cruise's streetwise girlfriend chimes in.

Some places reek of money. Others don't and never will.

How can you tell? What are the tip-offs?

Look at the cars in the parking lot. See Porsches, Ferraris, and other exotics? Unless the owners are trying to downplay their wealth or are subscribing to an ecological agenda, there will be a correlation between the value of the metal and the earnings of employees.

How are people dressed? In this ultracasual day and age, this is not a definite cue, but it isn't altogether off the mark either. Look at their shoes. Well made? Fashionable or enduring Brooks Brothers styling?

I did a major consulting program at a mutual-fund company. I made a ton of dough, and I stayed by the month in an apartment at the Four Seasons Hotel. A former U.S. president had a similar unit in the building. My suits were made in London.

A few years later, someone from that company phoned me to tell me about an opportunity to consult at a major insurance company. He said he never forgot the suit I was wearing when I ran a seminar that he had attended long before. That suit was valued at a few thousand dollars, but the impression it left earned me another half million.

You can take a few things from this story. Dressing well is an indication that people are earning well at a given company. Plus, it pays to dress well.

Let's get back to the win-win personality. This individual wants to associate with other successful people. If he's the boss, he'll share enough of the wealth to clone himself—to help others share in some of his style and the trappings of success.

Before I was at that mutual-fund company, I consulted for another firm. A fellow who knew that I earned pretty well took me aside. He pointed out that my navy blazer and gray slacks weren't going to cut it at that firm.

"Everyone wears suits here," he whispered. During my next visit, I wore a designer Italian outfit. Then I took several trips to London and stocked up with my favorite threads.

Note the point. I was pulled aside and clued in. If I wanted to justify earning the bigger bucks, I had to look the part.

The neighborhood in which a business is located will tell you a lot. Recently I passed on affiliating with two firms in the greater Los Angeles area. (I may offend someone with this comment, but that's life.) One is located in an ugly part of Culver City. CC is home to some movie and TV studios, so some of it is upscale, but the part that I researched was ugly and treeless. I could not imagine taking a single meeting there. The other spot was in the mid-Wilshire area, which fifty years ago was a hotspot. Today it is low-rent digs for various companies.

Robert Schuller, the late pastor of the Crystal Cathedral, said in one of his best-selling books, "Surround yourself with beauty."

Why? Because it is practical. It inspires us to perform better.

By the same token, ugliness is uninspiring. It takes the wind out of your sails.

Not to press the point, but I hesitate to work in areas where my car isn't safe. It is a very nice one. I don't want it vandalized or stolen. I want to feel safe where I work.

Surround yourself with winners. Work where winners work, and live where winners live. Don't apologize for having first-class tastes. Remember the old adage: birds of a feather flock together. You need to put yourself into a win-win context.

Is it possible to win when surrounded by losers and to feel good amid squalor and deprivation? I suppose, but why would you want to?

You're absorbing this information because you want to earn far more than you're used to earning. This means you have to change your existing outlook and environment.

Winners are also supportive communicators. They use ample praise. They see the good. They're optimistic. They're resilient. If they're fans of a team that has just suffered a disappointing season, they're the first to beam, "Wait till next year!"

I had a boss at Time-Life who was great in this regard. He'd come into the office and put a big grin on his face and exclaim, "Hi Gary!" It was over-the-top, but Larry was fun in this way. He nudged people out of their shells, making them act like extraverts even if they were introverts.

This is a crucial skill if you're running a sales office, which was his responsibility. He was a winner and he wanted everyone to feel like one. That's a win-win, supportive personality.

Supportive communicators do six things: They describe what needs to be done. They act empathically. They volunteer help. They're open. They share information. They don't blame.

Defensive communicators are different. They are likely to produce lose-lose outcomes. They evaluate and blame. They are guarded and closed off. They ration information. They're argumentative and off-putting. They expect people to do everything by themselves. They act in a superior and indifferent manner.

You have to ask yourself, why would I want to spend any time in that sort of person's presence?

Being an employer doesn't justify a toxic personality. Furthermore, I believe it is a thousand times harder to prosper with win-lose and lose-lose personalities than it is with win-winners.

Once I had a house next to the forest. A glass-and-beam wonder, this architect-designed perch was a unique place. On paper, it was worth every penny of its astronomical price, but down on the ground, it was very weird. Lots of snakes (one is too many for me). Foxes and deer frequented the backyard. Huge, ominous paw prints next to the swimming pool signified the presence of mountain lions. We heard thumping noises on the roof at night, and our bedroom was made of floor-to-ceiling glass—not a significant barrier to bears. Every chance we got, we drove an hour and a half to the Central Coast beach that we were very fond of. Finally we moved there.

Jobs and employers are a lot like that house. Even if it is a great position on paper, in the real world it can be a living nightmare. Moreover, your costs of escape can be astronomical. They're like a huge tax that we pay to avoid being where we are.

I knew a fellow in the Northwest who seized every opportunity to be on his yacht. It wasn't so much that he loved the boat. He couldn't stand the city where he was posted, so the only respite he found was on the water. Making big money is a waste if you hate the place where you're earning it.

Through these examples, I'm saying that the emotional cost of making the dough could be so high that it makes no sense to do it. The boss who pays you a premium but calls and texts you incessantly on weekends is no bargain. You *can* put up with such inconveniences, but not for long enough.

There have been times when I have made exceptional money, and I've enjoyed the process. But I've also treated myself to several miniretirements.

In my early thirties, I put myself through law school. Although I had my doctorate and had been using it professionally, law school was another mountain to climb. Taking into account the study required to take and pass the state bar exam, it took four years to complete the process. I suppose you could say that I semiretired. I accepted consulting work only when and where it wouldn't prevent me from attending the required classes.

To me, that's wealth. I worked, made great money, set another life goal, and paid for it in cash. No student loans were required!

One of my clients during the law-school years said something very pertinent to this discussion: "Life is too short to deal with unpleasant people." Defensive people are very unpleasant. They're unlikely to be able to create an environment where you'll be paid exceptionally well or have the resulting peace of mind to enjoy it.

Select win-win people to work with. Sometimes we can identify them in advance. They'll clue you in that the company pays exceptionally well, or that people move on to great careers after putting in a little time there. They may speak of work and life balance. They expect you to have outside interests and to want the time to pursue them. These are good signs.

In other cases, you may find that you're in a lose-lose setting. Companies that withdraw perks, cut back earnings, and feel as if they are shrinking away are not for you. Ditch them.

Do You Sincerely Want to Be Rich?

Bernie Cornfeld was the founder of an investment company a number of years ago. He coined this question: *Do you sincerely want to be rich?*

This is a crucial question for you to answer. I know you're interested in getting paid far more than you're worth. This is why were together at this moment.

Why do you want these excess funds? So you won't have to worry about money anymore? To become rich? To spend and buy? To say someone paid you far more than you're worth? To commemorate the fact that you're getting ahead of the game? To feel an ego surge from these accomplishments?

These motivations are all OK. I have no problem with them. They may be perfectly suitable for you. But you need to know why you're pursuing *more*. *More* won't happen by itself. The default setting of 99.99 percent of companies is to pay you less. Indeed they want you to earn far less than you're worth. Their objective is cost containment: keeping a lid on salaries and perks for folks like you. They know exactly what they want and why they want it.

A while ago I came across a fun book called *The Money Personality* by Dr. Sidney Lecker. He made several important points. One is the fact that we need to learn how to handle the mental game of earning more and getting rich.

Some people seem born with a winning predisposition. They pursue *more* without any regret or guilt. Instead of worrying that they'll lose all of their drinking buddies if they buckle down and aim at success, money personalities—MPs, as Lecker terms them—set bold goals and diligently pursue them, eschewing the predictable distractions that will get in the way.

More, or if you prefer, financial advancement, needs to become a primary objective, especially if you want to ear far more right away. I've already discussed how people can get rich their own way, but this takes a lot longer.

Spiking your earnings right now takes drive, like the rocket fuel that propels space voyages. We need to blast off. We need controlled combustion and thrust.

In pursuing more now, impatience is your friend.

Let me give you an analogy. One of my children is a nudger. A meal will begin, and right away she's asking about dessert. We'll be on our way to a museum, and, knowing the route she'll ask, "Are we going to the fish restaurant?"

Although she seems obsessed with food, her objectives are more diversified. She wants to repeat receiving perceived entitlements while lining up other improvements. Remembering our recent visit to Rome, she's now asking, "Are we going to Greece next?" She's seven years old, but she's already shaping the family agenda.

You need to become a nudger too. Nudge yourself into raising your aspirations. For instance, set a numerical goal:

"I intend to earn X money by Y time."

I made one of those pacts with myself. My goal was how much net worth I wanted to have by age thirty. It was ambitious, I'll tell you. While I'd love to say I hit it on the head, I didn't. I was thirty-three when I reached that number. But it guided my pursuit and motivated me, because it was a milestone, clearly delineated in advance, something I vowed to myself I'd pursue.

As I've already pointed out, I sought to achieve three to four times the income I was earning as a college professor. I beat that many times over, but the goal was important. It made it easy to devise a path to success.

Do you sincerely want to be rich? This is the question I initially asked. Then how much constitutes *rich* for you? You want to earn far more than what you're worth? OK: how much are you worth now?

Your reply could be exactly what you're being paid. It could amount to what you would be paid with your current level of experience and education if you were employed. Write than number down.

How much do you want to top that by? You can express it as a percentage, as I did, or you can write down a specific amount of currency. Alternatively, you can posit the acquisition of a certain item. You could say you want to earn enough to afford a monthly payment, insurance, taxes, and maintenance on a certain exotic sports car. Or you want enough to comfortably pay the rent or mortgage on a house at the beach, in the mountains, or in another wonderful locale.

Designating your *far more* goal this way has strengths and drawbacks. A plus would be the fact that you can garner that house or car in various ways. You could house-sit for some ultrawealthy people who own dozens of wonderful homes around the world. You could earn like a pauper but live like a prince, on a fraction of the income required to pay for such a place in currency.

Likewise, you could make leasing that car part of your executive compensation at a company or even at a nonprofit organization. Maybe you could convince a wealthy donor or car manufacturer to donate that auto, and you would have the use of it.

The drawback of saying you want far more as embodied in a product is that it isn't clear from the outset exactly how much you need to earn, if you're paying for it the conventional way, in currency.

Being numerically precise about your goal makes it more realistic. You can measure your progress along the way against a clear goal, and you can more easily plot an estimated time of arrival for its delivery.

The next question I have for you is this: assuming you sincerely want to earn far more than you're worth, what are you willing to give up to do it? To put it differently, what are you OK with delaying, ignoring, or putting in a second position with regard to your goals?

I earned far more as a consultant than I did as a college professor, but at what cost? For one thing, I slept in my own bed a lot less often. My professor Peter F. Drucker said, "Being a consultant means your work is always where you aren't!" Or as a famous columnist put it, "A consultant is an ordinary person more than 100 miles from home."

Being away as much as I was took a toll. I gained weight from the easy availability of rich food and drink. Upgrades to first-class on airlines alone offered far too many temptations to overindulge. I required a lot of down time to recuperate after being on extended consulting projects in remote locations. My pets were frequent guests at doggie hotels.

But to me, it was worth it. I learned a lot, and I was able to do much more with the batches of bucks I brought in. I would have been much less in charge of my finances if I didn't travel.

High income, in other words, was a primary gain. Many other things became secondary gains for me.

Do you sincerely want to get far more than you're worth?

Be prepared to make tradeoffs. Nothing is free.

Well, almost nothing. Recently I read about a financial firm in the state of Washington that was garnering headlines. The president decided to pay everyone a minimum of $70,000 per year. People who may have been earning half or less woke up one day to find that their income had doubled. They were earning far more than they were worth. Of course the company was flooded with employment applications.

Not everything was rosy. Some long-term staffers quit, feeling that many people were undeserving of such a windfall. Certain clients of this firm defected. They didn't like the politics of giving away money.

Unlikely as it is, you just might find an exceptional company such as this one in which to work. Even making an average contribution, you will be awarded with far more pay than you'd get somewhere else, but these situations are rare.

You have to sincerely want more and hatch a plan to earn it. It cannot be a secondary concern for you. It has to be primary.

Nonverbal Hints for
Earning Exceptional Money

Anthropologist Edward T. Hall famously said, "Time talks and space speaks." He was making a groundbreaking contribution to our understanding of nonverbal communication. Hall selected two variables to focus on: time and space. These two, he said, are culturally bound. People use time and space differently across the planet.

Companies have cultures as well. In our workplaces we need to determine what nonverbal behaviors need to be emulated. Mostly by following, but occasionally by breaking, these unstated rules, we can thrive.

For example, when I was in college, I grew a beard. This was not atypical of someone of my age, but it was also a message that I was deliberately sending. It made me look older and more mature, so I was taken seriously. It also made me appear to be academic, a thinker, a smart guy. Most of my professors were political liberals, and the beard looked a little left of center. They could identify with me. Having this image didn't hurt my grade-point average or my progress through graduate school.

One major hurdle we face as communicators is creating a sense of commonality. We do this by speaking, of course. When we discover that others have similar or the same interests, attitudes, beliefs, and values, we bond with them.

Let's say look at managers. When it comes time to recommend staff for raises and promotions, guess who will typically get the nod. It will be those with whom managers identify the most. We'll spiff those that are perceived to be like us.

This impulse, taken to an extreme, induces people to act prejudicially. That's not good. But arguably, there will always be bias in the workplace, and much of it is unconscious and from a practical standpoint unavoidable. Managers will succumb to such biases, and those that are favored by it have no reason to complain.

I've been both a fair-haired boy and a pariah in different organizations at different times. Believe me, it is a lot more pleasant to be favored than to feel you're being run out of town on a rail. You want to manipulate components of your image that meld into what your managers believe is an ideal employee, one that merits far more pay than he or she is worth.

Let's revisit Hall's variables—time and space. At some places, punctuality is essential. In fact, it is so significant that it receives unusual attention. Those that honor the clock are rewarded, and those that do not are punished disproportionately.

As an academic, I was used to being up to perhaps fifteen minutes overdue, especially in academia. The absent-minded professor stereotype supported this habit. After all, if your head is in the clouds, thinking grand thoughts, how can you be expected to be watching the clock? This logic also supported going over a class's scheduled meeting time.

The U.S. Navy cured me. It is the most time-conscious organization I've worked in. The Navy allowed no lateness and no excuses. If I wanted to work for this outfit, I was told very explicitly that I'd have to comply.

This order changed my behavior. To this day, I cringe and beat myself up if I think I'm going to a minute late in starting or concluding a class or a meeting.

Time talks, said Hall, and your use of it speaks volumes about whether you're fitting into a given workplace.

It's not only about being punctual. There are circumstances where being fashionably late wins the day. Sometimes working the clock the other way sends a signal that you have higher social or organizational status.

I know commission salespeople that refuse to keep predictable hours. Their use of the clock says, "I'm not paid to punch one!" If you know salespeople as I do, you'll recognize this attitude right away. They're "Don't fence me in!" types, preferring to roam wherever and whenever they please.

Their rationale is simple. They earn their keep by closing deals, by being effective, and not necessarily by being efficient. Effectiveness, by the way, is defined as doing the right thing. Knowing when and how to close deals, answer objections, and create urgency are typical skills of sellers. Effective sellers do these well. Efficiency, by contrast, is doing things right. This means dotting the I's and crossing the T's.

You need to know this, because exceptional earners are typically people that are paid to be effective. Professionals such as doctors and lawyers are called on to do the right thing, to make proper diagnoses, to choose the best solutions to address problems. If they're running late at the office because of their patient load, they're mostly forgiven.

I'm an author. If my books, audios, and videos have a good effect on my audiences, then I succeed. It is of little concern that my manuscripts contain 40,000 words or 50,000. I don't sell them by the word, and you don't purchase because of word count.

Let's talk about Hall's second observation: that space speaks. Take a look at your desk. Is it piled high with various items? This could be a plus if you are a researcher and you need to read original manuscripts. But most modern executives have very little on their desks. This sends a message that they are great organizers. It inspires confidence.

Where do you choose to sit when you're in a conference room? Do you sit at the head of the table? Higher-status and higher-earning people do. Does their power make them choose power seats? Or do they gain power by selecting these seats? The answer is, both.

By the same token, do what you can to become the wingman or woman of the top gun. Sit next to people with the clout. For one thing, you'll get into the visual field of everyone in the room. As they gaze his or her way, they'll be gazing your way too. This may sound trivial, but the fact is the more people see you, even bumping into you informally, the more comfortable they become in your presence.

Social scientists call this rate of encounter *serendipity*. It appears as a chance engagement of someone else's attention. You can and should make these things intentional.

When I was transitioning into my own seminar and consulting practice, the academic year was coming to a close. I had been ramping up my public-relations activities, sending out news releases by the dozen to regional newspapers.

One morning a colleague mentioned that he "ran into" me three times. He saw a leading article in the *Indianapolis Star-News*. He also saw a front-page article about me in the local paper. And he received a catalogue from an area university that was advertising one of my classes.

A few years later, I had an aggressive publishing program underway. I got six books out and into bookstores within five years. People browsing the stacks would happen along a large number of my titles at the same time. This made me seem to be the leading authority in my field.

I did a direct-mail campaign to promote my public seminars. Reaching out to thousands of companies, I sent about five circulars to each one. These were addressed to functions, such as sales manager, customer-service manager, and vice president of operations.

One person who attended my seminar and later invited me to speak to her company said she received multiple mentions of me almost simultaneously. "Different people put your flyer on my desk!" she beamed. She was completely unaware that my saturation campaign was intentional.

These examples show that it pays to get a lot of attention. If this attention can be focused within a short period of time, that's all to the good.

If you want to make your presence known to different units in your company (always a good idea), find ways to get your name and face in front of these people.

You might get permission to write an interdepartmental newsletter. Perhaps you can form a committee to coordinate affairs of common interest. After achieving this sort of exposure, you'll be in a position to hear which jobs are opening. When you apply, you'll have the sort of name recognition and credibility that will almost ensure your successful candidacy.

By running into people over and again, you have the effect of shrinking the space between you. They feel close to you, even if you haven't spoken many words to each other.

Clothing is also laden with credibility cues. As I've pointed out, one of my London-tailored blue pinstripe suits earned me about a million dollars in consulting fees. It impressed the right people in a top financial company. They hired me and referred me to another great client.

People don't wear their homes or their cars on their backs. They may not be visible enough to send a status message to percipients. But your clothes are a walking billboard that advertises your place in the pecking order. They signal your value and subtly say, "Pay me in a manner consistent with my attire."

A personal example, if you'll permit me. Sometimes, after a hard day of teaching the kids, my wife will "invite" me to dinner out. She'll dress up in one of her snazziest dresses and she'll purr, "Would you like to go out to dinner?"

She knows we're not going for fast food, and so do I. Who would waste such a lovely dress on McDonald's?

Clothing imparts messages. Choose yours carefully.

Some researchers suggest dressing up to the next rung on the organizational ladder. If you're a customer-service rep, you wouldn't bum it, even of the formal dress code permits casual attire. You'd deliberately dress like the customer-service manager. In this way, you'd separate yourself from the pack and seem like the second in command.

Nonverbal message sending and interpretation are critical to the overall communication process, but we're only marginally aware of its impacts.

Sociologist Erving Goffman says there are non-verbal expressions *given* and expressions *given-off.* The given kind is intentional. We smile when we see the boss, because we seek favor. But when we aren't trying to impress, our faces relax and sometimes settle into frowns or expressions of discomfort. These are expressions *given-off*: they are unintended. Often these get us into trouble. People may surmise that we dislike them and build an entire mental narrative around the idea that they should return the favor. Misunderstandings can result that are injurious to your income and your career.

"Face-work," according to Goffman, is required to get the most out of our interactions. This includes smiling at people, making them feel you like them.

Why would we do this, even if we're in a dismal mood?

I asked a psychologist what he thought the secret was to getting others to like us.

His reply: "Like them first."

We like people who seem to like us. As I said earlier, we favor these friends with better positions, more money, and an easier path at work.

Smiling is one of the most important nonverbal cues because it sends the message of liking. It's easy to do. If you are really uncomfortable with this fact of life, you should talk yourself out of having that feeling.

Some say it's phony to smile when we don't feel happy or pleased, but I see smiling as good manners. If you are hosting a party and guests are arriving, do you think part of your job is to put them at ease? I do, and this requires putting out the nonverbal welcome mat.

On another level, smiling works much like the Golden Rule: do unto others as we would have them do unto us. Smile at them if you want to be smiled at yourself.

To get back to manners, Peter F. Drucker said on many occasions, "Manners aren't about sincerity. They're lubricating oil, and they make social interaction happen with less friction."

Nonverbal communication research says the great majority, perhaps 80 percent or more of the messages people get and send, are word-free. It behooves us to become more sensitive to this hidden iceberg of meaning and to tap it for our professional benefit.

Subsidies Are Better
to Receive than to Give

In the depths of the last recession, a disturbing trend surfaced in companies. Instead of paying better and better wages, they headed the wrong way. Not only were they cost cutting, which meant hacking well-paying jobs, they were doing something even more insidious.

These companies were charging people money for the privilege of working for them.

Imagine securing a position somewhere, but instead of having them pay you, you pay them!

This odd "opportunity" that was spreading was called an *internship*. Recent college graduates were among others hat fell victim to this scheme. Desperate to get their feet in the door, baccalaureates would sign up with an employment agency, paying them money, to have that outfit sell the students into servitude. Students worked for nothing, which is just another way of saying they signed over their fair market value, which would normally be expressed in paychecks.

Colleges and universities are also in the slave-labor racket. They offer college credits to students who work in organizations without pay. Those college credits cost money, so students are out of pocket twice. They don't earn on the job, and they have to pay the college as well.

Colleges don't mind. You won't find them complaining. After all, they have outsourced the supervision, grading, and teaching of their students to companies, while they pocket the tuition dollars.

Yes, some of these slaves are hired later by the same companies. But there is an anchor on their starting incomes. A short time before, these companies obtained the students' services for free. Having enjoyed the milk gratis, those beneficiaries don't want to start paying the cow anything, so they'll part with the minimum they can get away with.

Internships are subsidies, plain and simple. They are giveaways that companies are only too happy to accept. In fact, they probably wish everyone were a volunteer laborer (except the CEOs, of course).

By the way, certain companies are set up as non-profit organizations, even though they look, act, and feel like private enterprises. Auto clubs are typically not-for-profit. There is a huge publisher, which offers exceedingly pricey seminars, that is also set up this way.

If you're looking to be paid more than you're worth, I'd suggest avoiding these odd ducklings. They'll defer, decline, or trivialize your requests for better pay and promotions by shrugging their shoulders and saying, "Hey, what do you expect? We're nonprofit!" But their senior executives never miss their pay raises, rich retirement plans, and other perks.

A famous philosopher pointed out, "If people are asking you to sacrifice, beware. There are always those that will be picking up your sacrificial offerings." Usually it will be those same folks.

Be alert to any and all requests for you to subordinate your interests on the job for the greater good. These overtures are trying to induce you into providing subsidies. *These sacrifices on your part will not be rewarded!*

Putting in countless hours of overtime is also a subsidy, and an obvious one, though it is often accompanied by rationalizations. For instance, new lawyers hired by large, prestigious firms may be paid a low six-figure income. On paper, this looks great, far above what they might have been earning before or during law school.

But the same lawyers are expected to bill 2,400 hours per year. An attorney works many more hours than he or she can bill for. If you do the math, this means they have to put in 70–80 hours per week. They're working two jobs in one. That six-figure income, while it sounds good, represents a far smaller hourly wage than these professionals expected to earn.

Is it worth it, when you calculate all the stress it entails to bill the required hours? Many say no after a year or two. After the tax bite on a higher income, and the nanny's or babysitter's payouts, there isn't much of that high income left.

Here's the truth of it: either you are subsidizing them or they are subsidizing you! It's far better to make sure you are receiving instead of giving.

What kinds of subsidies can they give you? This is a practical question, which we'll address, but it is also a question you need to ask, at least silently, each and every day of your employment.

Lots of employees leave money on the table, completely unaware of what they're doing. For instance, your

company may have an educational benefit that all workers can access. Sometimes this runs into many thousands
of dollars per year. Over the course of a career, it can
easily dip into the six figures.

If you have a BA, your firm may pay for you to earn
an MA or an MBA. If you don't have a degree, they can
very well pay for you to obtain your first.

This benefit is a boon in many ways. First, by applying for the funding, you're sending a message that
you're seriously interested in personal and professional
improvement. This will set you apart from the spuds
that simply want to kick back and watch 500 channels
of TV while emptying a six-pack every night. Your
accumulation of credits and certificates or degrees will
qualify you for bigger, better, and more frequent raises
and promotions.

Of course, the company will be paying all or at
least some of the cost. Typically you are not taxed on
this income. The company isn't either, because it is an
employee-training benefit. That's a win-win outcome.

The company may cut you some slack and let you
apply for a job that requires a degree if they can see
you're making progress toward earning one. They might
not make that exception for you if you're busy watching
Netflix when you could be in class.

"Do you know how old I'll be when I earn my
degree?" you might gripe. Do you know how old you'll
be if you don't?

"How will I find the energy to do this?" you may
wonder. Believe me, by stimulating your mind, having

deadlines to meet, and interacting with others, the process will give you energy, not take it away.

As you know, innumerable colleges and universities offer degree programs completely online. So the costs and inconveniences and time sunk into commuting to a location after work don't have to daunt you.

One of the best aspects of taking advantage of the educational benefit is that it will increase your marketability to other companies. They'll see that your current firm invested in you. Nobody does that with losers. And the new employer will be able to harvest your enhanced skills without having to invest in their achievement.

I've been mostly speaking of the big enchilada here—earning full degrees—and of course, this is a serious option, providing there is an ample subsidy. But you can take courses through university extension programs that culminate in certificates. These are serious credentials that also set you apart from your competition at work and in the labor force at large. Certificate programs often fill a gap in your background. They can also qualify you for new occupations and job titles. They can be completed in a fraction of the time required to do a degree.

Employers may also subsidize your attendance at trade shows and industry conventions. These functions provide professional training and seminars from which you will benefit. Your knowledge will grow, and you'll come back refreshed. Attendance at these meetings will also introduce you to contacts. You'll be able to add to your network, and these new people in your life will be sources of yet more job opportunities and better income.

I don't see a down side to taking advantage of this benefit. And if your company is like so many that want you to subsidize them by working way too many hours, you can always opt out.

"Gee, I wish I could stay, but I have class. Got to go!"

Some employers bring training sessions and even college credit-bearing courses to their own facilities. You'd be a fool not to take advantage of these offerings. Ask human resources to notify you of any and all available opportunities of this type. Simply by mentioning your interest, you'll be perceived as a go-getter, to use an old fashioned term.

Don't think for a minute that you're doing something noble by forfeiting any of your company benefits. You aren't. I just mentioned human resources. Those folks invested many personnel hours in devising a menu of employee benefits. Believe me, they're thrilled to see someone taking advantage. It validates their efforts, mission, and value to the company. Your supervisor may also derive enhanced credibility by having a self-improver on his or her team.

In the grand scheme of things, your participation may help your employer to become one of those firms that are regarded as the best companies to work for. This will enable it to recruit and retain more good workers like you.

If your employer has a vanpool operation, this is yet another way to give yourself a big raise. The costs associated with buying, leasing, maintaining, fueling, and insuring a car are huge. Typically, having a car can cost you $500 to $1,000 a month. That's income that could go directly into savings or investments, where you could enjoy compounded returns. If your firm doesn't offer a vanpool, ask them to inaugurate one! Everything has to start somewhere.

Human resources may have established relationships with numerous vendors. You may be able to purchase tires, insurance, and even vacation packages at deep discounts.

Everything I'm mentioning is a subsidy. This means part or all of the cost is being paid by or somehow made more affordable because of your affiliation with a firm.

If a perk or a benefit doesn't yet exist, push for its adoption! Some companies are creating extended family-leave programs. These enable new parents and caregivers or care arrangers for elders to take the time to acquit themselves of these duties.

I just heard of a company that has approved an unlimited personal-leave program. I don't have all of the details, but it appears that a worker can gain permission to take a substantial chunk of time off, even for a sabbatical. Sabbaticals used to be the perks of professors and the elite. Every six or seven years, professionals are given either nine months or a year to do something else. For academics, this may be used to write a book or to teach abroad as a visiting lecturer. The idea is to enrich the person's professional knowledge and to refresh their perspectives.

I know someone that worked at Xerox. That company paid him to be a resident at Paolo Soleri's desert research center, Arcosanti. This was a fantastic experience for him. Why not work for companies that offer a perk such as this?

Google, according to a recent article I read, offers some pretty astonishing perks. These include free negotiation classes (a topic near and dear to me!) and massages at their desks. It isn't easy getting hired by Google, but why not try?

My friend who worked at Xerox has always been able to point to the fact that he was a Xeroid, as they called themselves. Being an alumnus of a great company is a distinction in itself. It operates very much like a subsidy, because subsequent employers seek out people with Google and other fine companies on their resumes. These new hires can be expected to earn far more than they're worth. This isn't based so much on their future promise as on the halo they earned by having worked for a celebrated firm.

Remember: either you are subsidizing a company or they are subsiding you. Make sure that you are the beneficiary instead of the impoverished donor.

Even the Worst Jobs Are Gifts

There is an old vaudeville expression that I saw in a *New York Times* article: "You're either appearing or you're disappearing."

I feel this way about writing books, articles, and scripts for recordings. I need to be engaged to feel I'm alive. I need to contribute, and I appreciate feeling needed, feeling that I'm helping people improve their careers and their lives. If I'm not appearing in print or in recordings, I'm disappearing.

The same principle applies to work of any kind. You don't have to be a performer, an artist, or a creative type to derive satisfaction from your work.

All work, providing it is honest, is good. It gives us something we need. Income, self-esteem, feedback from others, goals, a way to measure ourselves relative to our peers—all of these things and more are achieved through working.

Just look at what happens when people are given the mixed blessing of retirement at or before the customary age. Many wither, dither, and simply go off the deep end because they have nothing substantial to do. They miss work so much that they make work out of their leisure.

I read an article about a famous TV personality whose contract expired. What did his day consist of? He got up, read the papers, went to a local place for breakfast, and got his hair done at the stylist's *every day*. Without realizing it, he was readying himself to appear on screen, though he had no job that required his presence. My sense after reading this piece was that he'd have gladly paid a studio to put him back in front of the red light five days a week.

We've all heard about people that retire and then, bam, they're dead a few weeks or months later. What is that about?

I believe it points to the essential nature of having a job to do. Working isn't the only thing in life, to be sure. But it seems that way if you're unemployed!

Believe me. I've been in that spot during much of my career as a consultant. When you consult, especially if you're in your own practice, you're in between gigs an awful lot of the time. The reason for this is simple: you're not a typical employee.

If a company is like a baseball team, it will put on the field nine of its everyday players. They're on the payroll as full-timers.

Consultants are temps. We may be glorified, highly credible, well trained, and superexperienced in our fields, but we're still temporary. Like pinch hitters who come late to a game, we're expected to step to the plate and get a clutch hit, a game winner. There's a lot of pressure, and many of us thrive on it. We want to be those go-to people upon whom a lot depends. We dig the rush that comes from being in that spotlight. Then we're back to the bench for many innings and possibly many games after that great moment.

Actors face much the same situation. They only earn so many parts. If they're lucky and they snare good roles in plays that have a long run on Broadway or London's West End, they're in clover. They get a steady check while staying in the spotlight. But when the curtain falls for the final performance, they're back to zero. Everything they do is geared to earning the right to perform again. Working is a gift, and when they're employed, every day is Christmas.

This is a great attitude to cultivate.

If you've been seeking a job for a long time, or you have experienced the feast-and-famine cycles that I have, it's easier to summon gratitude for those times when we are working. It's not automatic, though. When times are lush, it's easy to forget the slim pickings that we're had to endure.

There is a story told about someone who was seeking enlightenment. He pursued guru after guru. Each had his or her take on reaching a state of bliss. Some advised the seeker to empty his mind. Others suggested he eliminate all expectations.

Finally the pilgrim happened upon the wisest sage of all. Instead of saying anything, he opened the man's palm and tucked an engraved medallion into it.

It read: "This too shall pass."

Please keep this in mind as you sell your labor and work products. As the Frank Sinatra tune "That's Life" points out, you may be "riding high in April and shot down in May."

That's life.

Be grateful for the work you have at any given time. If you exude an aura of appreciation for what you have, it will make the time pass with ease and delight.

You may be temporarily underpaid. That's life.

This too shall pass.

We all go through these phases.

William Shatner, best known for his role as Captain Kirk in *Star Trek*, is the embodiment of the right attitude in action.

Reportedly, after achieving some success, his career tanked. He was living in a truck with his family—not a glamorous situation. He decided to accept practically every acting offer that came his way, irrespective of what it paid.

The idea was to dig himself out of the funk he was in. Working all the time was his antidote to not working at all.

He succeeded.

Here is the interesting thing. He accepted a job as media pitchman for what was then an unknown online travel agency: Priceline. They paid him a modest amount of money, but they threw some company stock into the deal. That stock made him a multimillionaire.

He breeds horses in Kentucky when he isn't busy acting. And he's almost always busy, by choice and by habit. He is certainly the captain of his own fate at this point, and he's not living in a truck.

Work is a gift. You're probably heard the expression, "The harder I work, the luckier I get."

Many of the skills that I packed into my seminars came from the training I'd received at Time-Life many years before. And my performance abilities in front of those seminar groups issued from teaching hundreds of college students over the years.

If you ask most people who succeed in their careers how it happened, they'll give you a pretty simple answer. In retrospect, each step along the path seems logical and even necessary as it led to the next, and so forth. But prospectively, looking forward, it is often despairingly obscure. For the life of us, we cannot determine the sense in a particular job or task that we signed up for.

Don't worry about that.

Whatever you are working on, consider it a gift!

I was doing a high-profile consulting project in Houston, and frankly, it wasn't going that well. I shared my ideas in seminars. People listened, went back to their desks, and nothing changed. They weren't enacting my suggestions.

This was more than regrettable. One night, about two in the morning, I awoke from a fitful sleep. I needed to do something!

It hit me. My seminars were inadequate for eliciting the behavioral improvements I was calling for. Not only did I need to lead horses to water, I had to make them drink. Seminars gave them a map to the watering hole. I had to take the reins and walk them to it.

In those wee hours I had an epiphany. I would add one-on-one coaching to my regimen. Seminars would provide the introduction and overview to my new methods, but I'd personally guide each trainee to implement.

Long story short, this new sequence worked amazingly well. People did what I preached, and their company prospered. By adding one-on-one training, I tripled the amount of billable days that were required to do the program. This was not my primary motivation; I went to the new format to improve the results. Yet by modifying the program I was able to triple my pay.

Even more significantly, I then rolled out the improved training formula to other clients, and they enjoyed equivalent success with it. In this way, a very difficult assignment, one that made me lose sleep, transformed into a groundbreaking training design and soaring profits.

That Houston client gave me a huge gift. You could say that my attitude went from "You can't pay me enough to put up with this" to "Thanks so much for challenging me to improve my tools!"

Each intractable problem hides a breakthrough.

Let's say you're in a frustrating job. Doing it isn't easy—far from it. If you can tackle this difficulty, you can improve matters for everyone and earn far more than you're currently worth.

Mark was in this situation in his job. He sold business opportunities to first-time entrepreneurs. The fee charged was about $5,000. Typically, sellers such as Mark collected 10–20 percent as a down payment. The balance was carried on the company books for up to 12 months, with clients making a steady payment each month. Mark and his peers earned 15 percent commission on all collected dollars. This meant they would get $150 if people made a $1,000 down payment. Then Mark and the company would wait to be paid each month.

This is what made the job so frustrating. Few clients would make all 12 monthly payments. A few wouldn't even make their second payment. This cost Mark, his fellow sellers and the company far less money than anyone wanted.

There had to be a better way, Mark thought, and he devised one. Figuring everyone loves a bargain, he experimented. He gave new clients a choice. They could put 10–20 percent down and pay the regular $5,000 price.

Or they could pay in full immediately and achieve a 20 percent savings, paying only $4,000.

Within weeks, 60, 70, and then 80 percent of buyers were paying in full. The company gladly approved the discount scheme. In fact, it offered sellers a 20 percent commission on full-pays. This meant Mark and his pals could earn $800 per sale immediately instead of the typical $150 from a down payment. The company was able to detach itself from the outside collection agency that it used to badger slow-pays and no-pays. Cash flow was incredibly improved.

What's more, buyers experienced greater satisfaction with their new business opportunities. Because they had invested more from the get-go, they put out more effort. As a result, a greater proportion of clients prospered. This turned into a win for the seller, the company, and the clients. And it all sprang from the creativity of Mark, who was frustrated and unhappy with his circumstances.

As this story shows, instead of quitting at the first sign of difficulty, if you can solve some of the problems associated with the worst jobs, you will earn a handsome gift.

Chapter 5

How to Transition into Earning the Big Bucks

If you always do what you've always done, you'll always get what you always got. You've heard this adage, and it's true.

You won't get paid far more than you're worth without making some changes in how you do your personal business.

There are some typical and predictable ways we sabotage ourselves and our incomes. Our unwritten manual for conducting our personal and professional lives is at the root of most of our income limitations. This set of dos and don'ts is what I call our *personal system*. Like the operating system in an electronic device, it can be buggy. This means it works slowly and inefficiently. Sometimes it breaks down entirely.

Your task is to clean this personal system. Scan it for viruses. This is what we're going to do in this section.

The first flaw our scan of the personal system will find is false beliefs. These are generalizations about ourselves, other people, and our limitations, and possibilities.

You carry around certain money beliefs. Finish this sentence: "Money is the root of all"—what?

Money is the root of all good things, the root of positive opportunities, the root of creature comforts?

Of course not. Money is the root of all *evil*, correct?

If this is one of your core beliefs, do you think you'll feel free to pursue more bucks with equanimity and joy?

I doubt it. This bedrock belief will undermine your efforts as you try to improve your lot. For every step forward you take, you'll be likely to take a step backwards, and maybe two or three. You'll find yourself frustrated, never able to achieve real traction in pursuit of a higher income. Or if you do achieve it, you may suffer from money guilt and lose your income or wealth in short order. Money guilt is the feeling that you don't deserve what you've earned. Walking around with that idea will introduce you to a world of pickpockets and thieves.

You've heard about the fate of most folks who win the lottery, haven't you? Do they make prudent investments? Do they spend only a fraction of the dividends they earn on their winnings? No, they do the opposite, and they end up broke in record time.

It's weird, right? Here they did what they needed to do to win. They bought a lottery ticket. They watched for news of the winning numbers. They tendered their ticket and got their winnings. Then they ditched the money as a sinking ship ditches its cargo into the ocean.

Have you ever asked yourself why this happens over and again?

It happens because on a deep level they believe money is evil, and we run away from evil. Bad things will come to us.

John Steinbeck wrote a wonderful little novel that we were made to read in school: *The Pearl*. The action takes place in a poor seaside village, where a fisherman catches an oyster. It contained a large, brilliant pearl.

This unexpected bounty doesn't deliver a better life, but the opposite. The fisherman loses most of what he really loved in life, what really mattered most to him.

It's a tragedy, to be sure. A beautifully written book, it tells an ominous tale of what can happen if your circumstances suddenly change for the better.

I'm here to say those that win and lose lottery loot, or their own versions of pearls, have a deficient belief system. It simply cannot live with success, so it sabotages success.

Give yourself a check-up from the neck up, as Zig Ziglar used to recommend. What are your money beliefs?

If you think money is evil, how in the world will you be able to enthusiastically be paid far more than you're worth and actually enjoy or keep the surplus?

Fortunately, we can change our beliefs. Let's say you have identified this belief—that money is the root of all evil—as one that has valence for you. Ask yourself, what evidence do I have that this is true? And what evidence do I have that it *must* be this way for me?

You'll discover that you have scant evidence to support this dour perception. Next, choose to believe its opposite. "From now on, I choose to believe that money is a source of much of the good in the world."

Give yourself examples of people who have raised their families out of poverty. Consider billionaires such as Bill Gates and Warren Buffett, who have pledged much of their wealth to charitable organizations.

If you like, commit to tithing, if you like. Donate 10 percent of your increased income to a worthy cause or institution.

Trust me. It is simply not possible to maintain a negative view of money and to pursue its acquisition at the same time. Change this core belief, if it is negative. It is a critical part of your personal system.

You may hold another unproductive belief: if you want to earn more, you'll have to take on added responsibilities. You may think you're too young or immature to bear a greater burden. You could think you're too old and past the point where you want to add stresses and responsibilities.

Again, dispute these beliefs. "What tells me I'm too immature? What proof do I have? And why do I think any immaturity I may have shown in the past will surface now, given my current challenges?"

Your hesitation to earn more could really be based on fear. Some folks fear success. They believe that it is undeserved and that it is just a matter of time before they fail big-time. If they succeed now, they'll fail later. Why deal with that sort of emotional roller coaster when they can remain untainted by disappointments?

Billionaire Richard Branson has the answer, which I've already mentioned. He advises people to take positions they know they are not ready for, because they can figure them out after they start.

This thought leads us to another area where our personal system is flawed. We procrastinate. Most people delay asking for raises, bonuses, and various opportunities because they believe they aren't ready.

Branson is implying something incredibly important: most of us are *never* ready at the time opportunities emerge. If we are completely capable of doing a job, this means we have done the exact job before. Who wants to repeat himself? We grow by taking on new things.

Inevitably we'll reach a point where we don't have all the answers. This is why we learn to ask! To overcome the procrastination habit, I suggest focusing on the smallest possible thing you can do to accomplish an objective. If you need a job, promise yourself to scan just one online employment source today. Start with just one, not five or ten or twenty-five. Anyone can click on Careerbuilder, Monster, Indeed, Glassdoor, or LinkedIn. Note that I have not asked you to do anything else. Just open the application and scan what's there. It's highly likely you'll find a job or two that look interesting. You may mark them down or apply to them.

But this isn't your first objective. In order to overcome procrastinating, all you are requiring yourself to do is *one small thing* in furtherance of your goal.

My dad used to visit my Little League baseball games. When I was at bat, he'd call out, "It just takes *one*, Gary!" This has become a bit of a mantra for me. He was absolutely right. I needed to wait for my pitch, the one I could connect with. I had potentially unlimited chances to do this with every at-bat, providing I fouled off the pitches that weren't just right for me. It took just one suitable pitch to do my job. The chap on the mound could only throw one at a time. By focusing on the one thing we could do at a given moment, the game made progress, and so did we.

We procrastinate in part because we lose focus on the smallest thing that requires doing now. We daunt ourselves by looking at the entire product that needs to be delivered. We feel the full weight of that result.

But most things don't happen all of a sudden. It is said that a sculptor working in marble has to make perhaps a hundred small chipping movements before a small piece of marble will be removed. It looks as if the result happened suddenly, but it was not the last of the sculptor's movements that got the result. All the hundred small efforts were necessary.

I will make a short defense of procrastination. There are times that we hesitate to accomplish something because we unconsciously believe it isn't the right project for us. You may hesitate to apply for a job because you've done that kind of work before and you weren't gratified with it. Rather than face this fact, you pretend you're interested in the work, but you won't make substantial progress toward the goal. A part of you is pushing toward something. Another part is holding you back. This is called an *approach-avoidance conflict*.

Try to clear these out of your personal system. Ask, "What do I really feel about this task that is leading me to procrastinate?"

You may see that procrastinating isn't your real problem. You simply don't want to accomplish the goal of the exercise.

Perfectionism is also a tendency that can pollute our personal system. As a consultant, I hold myself back by being too perfectionistic. As I note in my book *Dr. Gary S. Goodman's 77 Best Practices in Negotiation*, I do not regret the deals that I have done. Few have been total losses for me. My regrets come from the deals or jobs that I refused to do. In most cases, something was missing that I blew out of proportion.

One company responded to my $250,000 proposal by saying their budget could only handle $100,000. Instead of telling myself, "OK, give them $100K's worth," I balked.

"To do it right, we need a bigger budget," I insisted. The result was no deal.

I was being perfectionistic. Partly I had been spoiled. I had been blessed with numerous clients who met my budgetary requirements without objection. I wasn't used to compromising.

Plus, I was lazy. Instead of asking, "How can I work within a $100K budget?" I dismissed the idea out of hand. This is perfectionism.

Today I realize that I could have started with their figure. Then, having shown success, I could have gone back to the well for additional funds, and they may have been forthcoming. If not, so what?

Everything leads to something else. For instance, I teach at two major universities. I suppose I am underpaid. I have been underpaid now for sixteen years at one place and for eight years at the other. The sheer longevity of these relationships has meant a lot to me. I like the affiliations, and I enjoy teaching. But if you add up all of the dollars I have been paid during this time, it actually comes to a tidy figure. I didn't foresee this at all when I signed on. I can also purchase discounted football tickets!

Judging from each seminar budget, I was not earning enough. I was shortsighted in that judgment. I've had a lot of other opportunities arise from the attendees.

In sum, to earn far more than you're worth and perpetuate the gains you have made, your personal system needs to be clear of obstacles. These include false beliefs and other bad habits, such as procrastination and perfectionism.

Examine what you're telling yourself that may be holding you back. Often you'll find there is a core belief to blame. For some, it is the idea that money is the root of all evil. Change the beliefs that don't work for you by asking why they must be true, and especially why they need to be valid for you now.

When you are free of these limitations, your income should rise inexorably upward!

Your Present Is Your Point of Power

One insidious aspect of the job hunt is the emphasis put on résumés and on having had the right experience to qualify for a given post.

"Have you earned the right to be considered for this job?" is the tacit question asked of every applicant. If you aren't fully qualified, you're put to shame.

But this is a trap, one of many that every better-income seeker needs to be aware of. No one is perfectly qualified for anything. If someone seems to be the perfect fit, it is probably an illusion.

We need only look to U.S. presidents to verify the fallacy that there is a perfect candidate. Up to his election as president, Lincoln lost almost every race that he ran in. Until he reached the Oval Office, he was a loser, just a country lawyer without any genuine claim to fame. But many think he was a courageous leader who kept the United States intact.

Yet comparing his résumé to that of his adversary, Senator Stephen Douglas, any right-thinking voter would have to prefer the distinguished senator. Oddly, voters found something to like about Lincoln, and the rest as they say, is history.

Résumés, in other words, are very poor predictors of who will perform well in a job. Don't succumb to the idea that yours has to be perfect. If you do, you'll negotiate against yourself. This is whittling down your sense of value before anyone has challenged it.

Other, even stranger traps are associated with résumés. Let's say that you were an effective customer-service representative over the course of three years and you put that on your résumé. What exactly does that qualify you to become in the mind of a hiring authority?

Undoubtedly you are qualified to do the job that you have already done well. That's a no-brainer, but you're past that now. Yet a hirer could look at your résumé and say you haven't had airline experience, or Internet experience, or show-business experience.

Yes, but how do you get experience in a field if you're barred from getting experience in it? This is the perennial conundrum faced by job seekers. How can you get experience if no one will give you experience?

Let's thicken the plot even more.

Hirers say they want you to have industry-specific experience, but what if that isn't the ideal background to have? What if they're wrong about what constitutes the ideal background for a job?

If an industry allows only insiders to move from firm to firm, this inbreeding will cause problems. Without fresh blood, there will be no fresh ideas, no deviations from existing norms to enhance survival for a company or an industry.

For example, right now there are jobs advertised in cloud computing. Instead of being located in a server where you are, or in your PC or device, software is located in the cloud somewhere else. Salesforce is a company that enables salespeople to access files from practically any computer anywhere in the world. Sellers don't have to use their own devices, and they can work remotely.

This was a great innovation—using the Internet to access a software program. Programs can be continuously updated by manufacturers without requiring installation by customers. Today it is common to see more and more applications using cloud software.

There are plenty of jobs specifying that they require cloud experience. This is a dumb requirement, because at this point most people have used cloud software of some kind or another. Email programs operate in the cloud. The emails we send and receive are archived in the cloud. They're not using memory space in our PCs.

Let's say I want to work for Salesforce, but I haven't worked for any cloud-based company. Why should my lack of cloud experience prevent me from qualifying for a post?

In other words, what is it about "cloudness" that I don't already understand that is so essential to performing well in most of their job openings? Unless I'm writing computer code—and even then—what is so special about the cloud anymore?

By the time you read this example, this cloud requirement may be as irrelevant as requiring that people be able to type forty words per minute. Everybody types. Yes, some are faster than others, but who hasn't used a keyboard in this day and age?

By the same token, who hasn't used cloud applications? Requiring this background is about as meaningful as saying, "Applicants must have breathing experience."

I believe a lot of these "insiders-only" job requirements are invented by clueless human-resources dum-
mies who have to put something down to give a job ad
some girth. Otherwise their listings would appear to
be too thin. And then the HR people would not have
enough to do to distinguish one résumé from the next.

Possibly a decade or two ago, before it became ubiquitous, cloud software was a hard sell. But the outdated job
requirement is still there, staring you in the face, making
you freeze up lest you apply for a post with which you
don't seem to be in strict conformity.

How do you handle this?

*In employment negotiations, like the game of horseshoes,
close enough is good enough.*

If cloud experience is required in a job you want, I
suggest you ignore this requirement and apply anyway.
In the interview, you can explain how your actual experience is the equivalent of cloud experience or persuade
them that your specific background is actually better.

Or you can fudge the requirement. Do you have
cloud experience? Yes, you do—as a user. No, you hav-
en't worked for a cloud software company as such, but
your have accessed plenty of things on the cloud. These
experiences have told you most of what you need to know
about cloudness. What you don't know that is essential
the firm will teach you, because they will have their own
unique take on what cloudness means.

Isn't fudging the same as lying? No, it isn't. You have
the right to emphasize anything you like while deem-
phasizing anything less relevant in your estimation. Hey,

the hirer fudged the pertinence of cloudness, didn't they? Turnabout is fair play.

Résumés and their devotees focus obsessively on the past. That's the wrong emphasis. What if you want someone new?

Résumé imprisonment won't unlock you from the past. It will keep you a captive of what you have been.

You need to shift the focus to what you can and must become.

For example, if you have been in customer service, it is time to move into sales. That is advancement, and it can be justified on the basis of your proven customer-handling capabilities. Sure, there will be questions about whether your passive role in getting calls will have prepared you to take an active role in making them. But you can counter that the phone works both ways, and you have made outbound contacts too. Besides, persuading upset customers in accepting suboptimal solutions is a sales job, and you've done well in it.

"Now I'm ready for this" or "Now I'm perfectly prepared to do that" is type of claim you should make.

The key here is that the present is your point of power, not the past.

They don't have a job to fill in the past. Something in real time needs to be addressed. Your interview, your cover letters, and your résumés need to establish this fact. *You're ready now.*

Emphasizing your past can lead you into other traps. For one thing, your best days may seem to be behind you. Their company may not measure up to the ones that you've been affiliated with. This could give rise to the question, "After all of that experience, why would she want to work for us?"

This sentiment is the kissing cousin to "You're overqualified." I believe this statement is bogus on lots of levels. There are three possibilities here: you're unqualified and never will be; you're almost qualified, and with a little training you'll be there; or you're qualified and can step into the open role immediately. Calling your overqualified is akin to saying, "You're too capable."

Say you need a cab to get you to the airport. The driver needs to be quick, safe, and familiar with the best route to accomplish the task. If on top of that, he has a sixth sense for danger, intuiting when others are going to make boneheaded moves, does that make him overqualified? What if he has a PhD in astrophysics as well? Does that make him overqualified?

No, it does not. It may qualify him for a teaching or research job in a pertinent field, but this does not decertify his cabbing capabilities.

Calling your overqualified is a label used by people looking for an excuse not to hire you. They can't say you're ineffective, because you have proven your effectiveness. So they say you're too good, meaning you'll somehow fall short. It makes no sense.

If you spend too much time pitching your past, which is what résumés induce you to do, you'll provide the kind of data that make you seem like a poor fit. Thus you need to pare away the irrelevant.

I saw a posting at LinkedIn that asked, "What can attorneys qualify for outside of the legal field?" I answered, "They qualify for anything, providing they don't disclose they're attorneys."

Networking for Superopportunities

When I was moving to a small college town to teach, I was on my own in finding a suitable apartment in which to live. The housing market was very tight by the time I hit town. All I could find was a nasty mildewed basement. I bailed on that place and got a unit above a house, but that place was infested with bees.

I had new courses to prepare, and I couldn't fight my environment at the same time. I decided to network for apartments. I needed to know what was coming onto the market before anyone else.

I called the advertising department of the local newspaper. I told them I was a new professor in town, and I needed suitable digs. Could they please give me a heads-up when they were about to advertise a new listing?

The person I spoke to said, "What a coincidence! My dad has an apartment in his home that will be coming up at the first of the month. Would you like his phone number?"

I called him, and we hit it off. The apartment turned out to be a great place on a beautiful, leafy street. That's where I lived for the duration of my academic year.

This episode illustrates the power of networking. Everybody knows somebody. The key is to put out the word that you're seeking a certain kind of position and get your friends, acquaintances, and even strangers to work for you.

What's in it for them? Well, some folks have a soft spot for a person in need. They feel good by doing good for others. Others may help because the law of reciprocity. They realize that you'll pay them back in kind when their time of need comes up. Still others may work for your cause because there is a direct benefit to them. They may have a family member who is looking to supply just what you need, as occurred to me with that apartment.

You may have heard the expression, "Networking is a contact sport!" It's true. You may be lucky and know someone who is extremely well connected.

I know someone at a local university who is like this. She knows other academic administrators and people at chambers of commerce, and most importantly, she'll gladly share their names and numbers with you. Like a good politician, she recognizes that her power and influence grow with each solid connection that others make with her help.

Don't think you're out of line to ask for help. Some of us are too proud. We believe, falsely, that our image suffers if we ask anybody for help. Somehow, being "needy" is inherently bad. Well, let me tell you a story.

I worked in a large financial firm and reported to the president of a division. I didn't like this person very much. When his unit was reorganized, and his command was given to someone I did like, I didn't complain. He probably knew there was no love lost between us, but he did something I respected. He called me and said, "You probably know that I'm looking for another position, and I was hoping you might tell your financial-industry contacts about me."

Believe me, that was not a top priority of mine, but if I did hear of something, I probably would have passed that information to him. Contacting me took guts. That's an admirable trait. After all, someone may not be a good fit in one situation but could be a perfect fit in another.

Networking works. But you have to work it hard to make it work for you.

Here are a few tips, some dos and don'ts.

Realize that some people will not help. This is normal and to be expected. If you ask them about opportunities at their current company, they may feel threatened.

I know a fellow who acts this way. I helped him to survive at one of his previous places of work. He wasn't getting sales, but I saw talent in him. I also saw that his confidence was shot, so I buttressed him and built him up. He responded and succeeded. Good for him.

When I noticed there was a position of interest to me at his future company, I reached out and asked him about it. It was senior to his title, and I'm sure it paid far more than his salary, but he knew I rated big pay. It would have been a feather in his cap to have brought me in. In some cases there are bounties paid, referral fees to be earned, for encouraging someone to come aboard.

Yet his support suddenly and inexplicably stopped. When I asked him for details about his firm, he became inaccessible. I sensed he may have felt threatened somehow.

Here I had a person that actually owed me a big favor but wouldn't come through.

You'll also find that others who barely know you will go out of their way for you.

You simply cannot predict where networking help will hail from. This is why you need to cast your networking net widely. As Ovid said, "Always keep your line cast, for in the most improbable of ponds, you will find a fish."

Talk to a lot of people. Tell them you're looking. Use the Law of Large Numbers.

Networking is really very similar to selling, but instead of pitching a product or service or even yourself, you're just *announcing*. You're announcing your availability and interest in finding an opportunity. It's that simple.

You can place a little bait on your hook by asking, "To your knowledge, who is hiring?"

If the person's employer is adding personnel, the odds are good you'll hear that. Again, they may earn a referral fee if you're hired. They may steer you to their brother-in-law's employer. You simply never know.

If they do give you a lead, you can follow with this question: "Who do you know there?" Get them talking. If they become interested in your welfare, they may suggest you speak to someone specific.

In a way, you're like a detective. You're seeking clues to a valuable opportunity. One question leads to another.

You share information about yourself, and the law of reciprocity induces others to share vital information with you. One individual leads you to another until you're speaking directly with an opportunity holder.

You might wonder about online networking sites. Can they help in your job hunt?

Undoubtedly they can. For instance, LinkedIn has a job-seeker package that you can sign up for. It enables you to send emails to lots of people. Most importantly, Linked In is a great list. Companies typically have their own pages. You can see what job openings they have. Even better, you can learn the names of some of their recruiters, the ones that have been retained to fill those openings. You may not see a job you like, but you should reach out to the recruiters. Network with them! If they like you, they'll visit your LinkedIn page. They may ask for your résumé. You can also ask them for the names of other recruiters that they know.

Another technique is to use a site like LinkedIn to determine where the jobs are. Let's say you want to work in software engineering. You live in Phoenix, so of course you look for jobs there.

But it's supersimple to search for software engineering jobs *everywhere*. Simply count the listings to see where the most promising job markets are. If you see a hundred listings in San Francisco, thirty in Los Angeles, and five in Phoenix, this might be a hint that you should consider relocating. You can also be assured that there is greater lateral and upward mobility in the San Francisco Bay Area than you'll find practically anywhere else in the country. Wherever there are lots of strong jobs, there are strong upward pressures on wages. You want to ride the crests of those waves.

Let's say you want to stay where you are. What do you do? There's nothing wrong with networking with those robust employers in the Bay Area for jobs that they know about in Phoenix.

You'll find the quality of jobs listed in LinkedIn to be better than what you'll find at numerous "free" employment sites. While there may be a little overlap, most of the LinkedIn jobs will be of a higher caliber and pay more than what you'll find at Monster, Careerbuilder, or Indeed.com.

Certain Employers May Not Be Good Enough for You

I've quit a number of jobs, and I've been fired too. Anyone that hasn't is simply inexperienced. Or they're lying to you.

Coming and going are as predictable as the tides. High tide, low tide, and in between, life and employment are always in motion.

But there is a myth of stability, of stasis. We internalize a belief that there is a perfect job out there waiting for us. It is our mission to find it. And then, by gosh, we should hang on to it with all our might.

If only that were true! But if marriages and families fall apart, why in the world should we believe that a job, which involves a mere economic relationship, should endure longer than our other associations?

The lifelong employer myth ranks up there with the Tooth Fairy. It's a sweet idea, but naive at best.

Your Grandpa Milt may have toiled on the assembly line for GM back in the 1960s, and he could have retired with a nice pension after twenty years. But that sort of gig is rare in today's world. Here's the truth of things in today's scene: employers are reluctantly bringing you aboard, and they're itching to replace you at their earliest convenience. This is true practically everywhere.

If there has ever been an occupation that should have been immune from such pressures, it should have been selling. When I was putting myself through college, one of my early and best bosses made this often repeated comment: "If you're a good salesman, you'll never be out of a job!"

In theory, this makes complete sense. Let's say there is a thriving company. They have top sellers that are doing well. Can they use another one? Naturally they can, and they also want to make sure their competitors don't get her.

Let's say there is a company that is in serious decline. They've been losing clients and market share. If they have a shot at hiring a superb seller who will bring in far more than he costs, will they decline? They may be in pain, but they aren't stupid.

As obvious and logical as these inferences are, we know from behavioral economics that people do not always act in their best interests. Simply being at the helm of a business doesn't make someone a perfectly rational being. They can make crazy decisions for crazy reasons. Much of the time their nuttiness evades review, and they keep doing what they're doing.

You've heard the wonderfully twisted adage, "No good deed goes unpunished," haven't you?

You can substitute one word, and this is just as true: no good *employee* goes unpunished.

Why?

Let's go back to that top seller. You would think companies would lavish all sorts of goodies on these rainmakers. "Please stay, and keep doing what you do" should be on their lips, at least when performance reviews come around. These performers should be celebrated, not derided.

What's more likely to happen? The sales manager (typically not a sales superstar in his or her own right) could be jealous.

This happened to my dad at one prestigious advertising company. His boss criticized him for earning big money. "It's embarrassing!" the supervisor exclaimed. "You earn more than I do!"

That's not an unusual situation for a premier seller. He or she will typically do that.

Sellers who regularly outperform their quotas are often the targets of pay cuts. Companies may halve their territories. Suddenly there are 50 percent fewer prospects in the rainmaker's universe. The justification is, "The territory's potential is much greater than what we're seeing."

Positive, productive behaviors are punished instead of being rewarded. You need to expect irrationality of this kind in companies, because managers and owners are neurotic. As Dostoevsky said about such characters, "They're in clover, but the clover isn't good enough."

Please don't think this bizarre behavior only victimizes salespeople. Everyone is subjected to it.

Companies need you, but they don't want to. If they had their druthers, they'd have zero employees. Employees are costs, and cost cutting reigns supreme.

You've heard a lot about artificial intelligence. This is about thinking machines that can replace humans. The buzz started with IBM's supercomputer, which learned to play chess. Pitted against chess masters, the machine fared well.

Fast forward several decades. Robots are performing surgeries.

What am I driving at? Companies don't want us. They never have, except as instruments of profit. If there are cheaper means of getting those profits, we'll all be shown the door.

Our days as employees are numbered. Middle-management ranks have already been hollowed out because of enterprise software. Unskilled services such as assembly-line work have already been largely reassigned to smart machines. Skilled labor (including that provided by lawyers) is being outsourced to other nations. Do people really need accountants to do their income taxes in an age of cheap software? I don't!

How will these trends affect your ability to earn far more than you're worth?

If you expect to work for others, you'll need to be nimble. Move quickly from one employer to the next in order to pyramid your income and benefits.

No matter what, do not permit yourself to get sentimental about any given employer. I've easily left a million dollars or more on the table because I stayed too long as a consultant at certain firms. I liked the people. I liked the money. I liked the Four Seasons Hotel where I rented a suite by the month. But I could have done even better if I realized what I'm telling you now.

There's no time to smell the corporate flowers.

If you're earning the big bucks, that's great. Take them and invest them. You'll need them later.

You may want to seriously consider opening your own firm. Speaking of CPAs, one of mine did this after working for a larger firm. Although they made him a partner, he had to live with their inefficiencies. They drove him off the deep end with their waste. He figured that he and a few others could start their own practice, bringing over a few clients and building from there.

He did well. He never looked back.

You can leverage and cash in on the skills you're learning by working for others. You may want to launch your own enterprise. One reason is the simple fact that you will never fire yourself, unless you feel you're growing incompetent. Then you can delegate your role or sell the business.

The problem in working for others is that you'll never be family; you'll always be an expendable member of their team.

Look into my book *The Forty-Plus Entrepreneur.* You'll see lots of good reasons for transitioning into a business of your own. I'll show you how to do it.

In the meantime, appreciate that you're worth far more than money, and employers simply don't deserve to underpay you.

Would You Invest in the Necktie Business Today?

When I was growing up, I thought neckties looked really cool. There was a drugstore (of all places) about a block from where I lived that had a necktie rack featuring radically discounted items. I bought some, even though at twelve or thirteen I didn't have many places where I could wear them. They were too cool to pass up. Today I have a number of designer ties, including a handful by Jerry Garcia, the late guitarist with the Grateful Dead.

Yet neckties are really going out of fashion, unless you follow a fashionista such as the late Karl Lagerfeld, whom I have never seen photographed without one. James Bond still wears one every so many movies.

But I have a question for you. In a time such as ours, when ties are no longer required at the office, do you think there's much of a future in this item? Seeing the trends at hand, would you invest your money in the necktie business?

What does this have to do with getting paid far more than you're worth?

Plenty, I believe.

When we work for a company, we're investing in it. Obviously we're investing our time and effort, and we're paid a certain amount for these contributions, but in the bigger scheme, we're selecting a firm and an industry to which we're hitching our career wagons. You need to ask yourself, are they worth my commitment today, and even more importantly, tomorrow?

Peter F. Drucker was fond of asking people this question: "Knowing what you do about your business, if you had the choice to enter it again today, would you?"

This is a penetrating probe. It forces the listener to make a profound judgment.

Many of us keep doing what we do out of inertia. "It's what I know best," some say. Others point to their education and experience relevant to the field.

For example, I am a licensed lawyer. I can practice anytime, and I can make this my main squeeze. But there has been a downtrend in the legal field since I passed the bar. I don't see the advantage in using this very expensive credential and license in the way most would.

Would I enter this field today, knowing what I know? Probably not.

Drucker went on to say if we wouldn't reenter the field today, we should probably get out as quickly as we can.

I've worked in firms that had some big troubles. Their industry may have been in decline. They may have been losing customers. The direction they were heading in was down.

You don't want to be the last to dive off a sinking ship. And you certainly don't want to step onto one for the first time when you can see it is taking on water.

Yet these companies do advertise for employees, partly because they've lost the people who have abandoned ship.

You need to research the companies you are thinking of joining. Scrutinize them as carefully as you would if you were investing your retirement funds in them.

Most industries go through three stages: market entry, growth, and decline.

Companies follow these stages too.

Take solar energy as an example. Not so long ago, the idea of harnessing solar for electrical needs was the stuff of science fiction. Today Germany is producing about 20 percent of its total power from alternative sources, such as solar, wind, and hydroelectricity.

As recently as five years ago, you could join a solar company in sales and easily earn a six-figure living. Solar was trendy to install, and early adopters with money or equity in their homes would take out a big loan to finance an expensive system. Many governments offered attractive tax incentives as well.

The market for solar energy is still growing, but practically everything has changed. System costs are declining because of technological innovation. Systems can be leased. Profit margins are declining because there are more providers. Heck, the other day I rode behind a plumbing truck advertising solar installations.

Would I hitch my wagon to the solar star today? The industry is well beyond the entry point. It is still in a growth mode, but there is also decline, especially in pricing power and in profits to be earned. The best-positioned companies may still be attractive employers, if only because they will be the biggest and the best-funded. They'll be able to withstand the forces of change and still profit.

As for the rest, the smaller ones, and the start-ups, would I join forces with them? I would not.

If you want to be paid far more than you are worth, you need to work with companies that are paid far more than THEY are worth!

These will be firms that are in the early to growth phases of their enterprises. In the 1967 film *The Graduate*, a well-meaning relative whispered to Dustin Hoffman where the future of business beckoned.

"Plastics!" he beamed to a nonplussed teenager who didn't see the excitement.

One of my neighbors did the same for me decades later when he urged me to consult for mutual funds. Quite by accident, I did so, and I earned a ton of dough.

You need to listen to these whisperings in the breeze to earn exceptional paychecks.

In 1993, I worked with a fellow at a software company. He said where he thought the world was headed. "The Internet," he whispered to me.

Today, for most of us, the Internet is as ubiquitous as water is to a fish. But at that time, who knew about the Internet?

Peter F. Drucker said no one can see the future. But we can see what has already occurred that others haven't recognized yet.

Plastics, mutual funds, the Internet—all of these existed, but only a few recognized how universal they would become.

I can tell you where the action is NOT. I am a student of employment ads. They indicate which companies are succeeding through growth and which are declining because of incessant turnover. Where you see the most ads, either of these things could be happening.

Right now, I detect a ton of ads coming from the merchant services area. These are companies that are selling credit-card processing. Their business model is pretty simple. They get a cut of all of the credit-card transactions that their clients do. Let's say they have a restaurant client. Every time a card is swiped at that restaurant, a little bit of profit accrues to the merchant services company.

A typical restaurant will have hundreds of transactions every day. Multiply this by hundreds or thousands of restaurants and other retailers, and you have a huge amount of income flowing in. Plus, these companies sell merchant cash advances, which are like high-interest loans. There are big profits to be made.

Looks like a great industry, correct? The problem is, it is flooded with new providers each day, and the only real difference between them is cost. This means there will be a shakeout and some big survivors. The time to have entered this business was years ago.

Either work for the biggest and best, or forget about it.

Yet merchant service companies are running ads, mainly for salespeople. Aren't they growing?

It's illusory. They hire sellers that are paid on commission only. If they line up a client, great—they earn a fee. If they don't make it, their employer quickly replaces them with two or three more bodies. It looks like growth, but if you are a seller, it feels more like desperation.

To earn your investment as an employee, a company needs to have a solid business advantage. A firm must compete on value. Competing on price cannot endure. If a firm competes on price, the salary they are cutting will be yours. It is very hard to justify getting a raise in a cost-cutting environment.

A firm that can afford to pay you far more than you are worth is one that is earning far more than they are paying you.

When I was an account executive for a Beverly Hills car-leasing firm, it was a great time to come aboard. Leasing was increasing in popularity. Beverly Hills was like an ongoing car show. People strutted like peacocks in their expensive rides. And the firm I joined had recently gone public. It had cash to acquire competitors, which it did very quickly. Account executives inherited customers instead of having to beat the bushes for them. We were given new cars to drive, car insurance, medical benefits, a decent salary, and commissions.

In their time of rapid growth, companies such as my leasing firm are *willing to overpay* to keep up with the demand they are creating.

Some well-funded technology start-ups are willing to do the same. They may have a potentially hot product and a very limited time to introduce it widely. They are willing to burn through bucks quickly to establish a customer base that will prove the efficacy of their product.

Part of their spending will be on you, to make you happy and productive. What they are losing by overpaying you and your peers pales in comparison to the now-or-never opportunity they have to establish their product in the marketplace. At this stage in their evolution, who cares if they pay you twice what you're worth? They'll recover those pennies millions upon millions of times over in terms of a high initial stock valuation.

Months or years down the line, the same companies will have human-resources departments that will crunch down salaries and perks. Maturing quickly, these companies will start to rein in costs in order to show a profit after the madcap growth subsides or the market introduces competitors.

But let's get back to my theme. You are an investor. Just as you would love to buy a cheap, hot stock that has a very high ceiling, you want to find a company that will earn a valuation far greater than it is actually worth. Joining them at that point in their evolution will provide you with far more income than you are worth.

Where are these companies?

As of this writing, many of them are in the San Francisco Bay Area. I train their people in my negotiation classes at UC Berkeley Extension. They jump from job to job at least every two years. Competition for capable people is intense, and there is always a bigger and better paycheck somewhere along the 101 freeway, in Silicon Valley, or in the East Bay. Friends recruit friends, and big referral bounties are paid to those that bring aboard effective people.

You may have heard not long ago that San Francisco has become the most expensive area to live in. Housing prices are off the charts. Many hear this and say they would prefer to be in a backwater. I understand, and there is much to be said in favor of cheap living, especially if you are earning far more than you need to meet it. But inflation is rocking San Francisco because people there are being paid far more than they're worth, and companies are thriving enough to issue those fatter paychecks.

Be nimble. Be willing to move from firm to firm as their fortunes, and yours, change. Be willing to move to different regions of the country or to other countries to earn far more than you're worth.

When you commit to getting more, you are also committing to exploiting incongruities. Professional investors are always seeking price incongruities. These are stocks that are cheap when compared to their actual value. As an investor in your own career, you need to find price incongruities as well. You are looking for companies that are willing to pay more than your value.

They are out there. Seek and you will find one.

Even if it isn't in the necktie business!

How to Stay Positive
about Earning Top Rewards

Their noses were pressed to the tour bus's windows as they rode by the mansion. Some jaws dropped, others smiled, and a few pointed at us.

My friends and I continued our football tosses, as the bus driver was undoubtedly announcing which movie stars' homes flanked the lawn on which we were playing.

A few years before, I could have been on that bus, if it had been carrying tourists from the Midwest. It was then that my family decided to leave Chicago heading for the sunny Pacific and the fantasy factory known as Beverly Hills, which was home to lots of film and TV stars and other celebrities. The winners of the world converged on that tiny triangle of turf.

What most people didn't know back then, and don't know even now, is that you didn't have to be rich or famous to live there.

John, the war-wounded newspaper vendor at Beverly and Wilshire, lived in a rented garage apartment on South Rexford, near Beverly Vista School. It was overgrown with bougainvillea and other vines, and you wouldn't know there was a doorway leading to his humble castle. He probably paid no more than a few hundred bucks for the place. But he enjoyed all of the benefits of any resident, including a respected and responsive police department, beautiful parks, and the other amenities you might expect from an upscale enclave.

Outsiders didn't realize that there are apartments and condos for rent in Beverly Hills for only a fraction more than these units would cost beyond the town's borders. Possibly you'd pay a 10 or 20 percent premium, but that was a bargain, especially if you had kids. The public schools were revered for being as good as, if not better than, most private schools. Going to them would save far more than the differential in living costs.

And those movie stars and celebrities I mentioned? At least half of their children attended the public schools with me. Talk about a small world. One of those celebrity kids was literally born next to me in a Chicago hospital. We found ourselves taking the same class at Beverly Hills High School fifteen years later.

I'm sharing this with you because you need to know that the goodies in life are yours for the taking if you put yourself into the right context. Remember the saying "Get to paradise and paradise will find a way to support you."

If you want to earn far more than you're worth, or at least live a lifestyle that is the equivalent, you need to adopt and maintain an appropriate mental attitude. In the case of Beverly Hills, each person that lived there, including John the news vendor, who earned the princely sum of 3 cents for each paper sold, believed he or she deserved it.

They gave themselves permission. They put themselves into the Beverly Hills picture.

When I was in the car-leasing business in Beverly Hills, I learned an important lesson about car values. The cost of a new car does not equal your cost of driving, even though we think it does. For instance, let's say you'd love to drive a Porsche (and I can tell you that is a good choice. I love mine). You might think a Porsche is too rich for your blood. It probably isn't, and I hope by the time you are earning far more than you're worth, you'll agree.

Anyway, the actual cost of a Porsche isn't the sticker price or what you agree to pay the dealer.

The cost is a function of how the car depreciates over the years. Say you buy a used Porsche for $50,000. You drive it for three years, and you sell it for $35,000. What has it cost you? Putting aside gas and insurance and the interest you paid, the Porsche cost $15,000, correct?

That is $15,000 divided by the 36 months you drove it. That comes to about $417 per month. How much is your car payment right now? Let's say is a very reasonable $295, but you're driving a plain vanilla vehicle. Wouldn't it be worth a little more than $100 a month to step up to a Porsche?

But there's something else you need to factor into the math. How is YOUR car depreciating? Let's say you bought it used for a modest $29,000. At the end of three years, let's say the market for it is soft, which isn't unusual for most cars. It will only bring $12,000. Your cost of driving for three years of use has been $17,000! That's actually $2,000 more for your vanilla vehicle than it would have cost to drive a Porsche!

These figures aren't intended to be spot-on, but they do make the point, which we saw every day in the leasing business. It could actually *save* you money to drive a more expensive car, and the smart folks knew this and exploited it.

I still abide by this insight. My cost of driving is really cheap, but my enjoyment of first-class vehicles is ongoing and incredibly affordable. If this sounds like eating your cake and having it too, that's exactly how it feels.

There are a few important beliefs that undergird my elite driving practices. First, I deserve to drive great cars. Second, I can drive great cars and minimize what they cost me. These beliefs are akin to what Beverly Hills residents tell themselves. They deserve to live there, and there are ways to live there at a fraction of what others pay or think they must pay.

You must tell yourself, "I deserve to earn far more than I am worth, and there are many ways to do it." This is part of the mind-set that you need to sustain when you aren't seeing any material progress toward your goal. It isn't always easy, but it is necessary.

How can you stay positive when you only experience seeming negatives and setbacks?

Do what actors do. They experience, arguably, more rejection and poorer results than practically any other occupation. I know some pros who have had break-throughs, landing ongoing roles in TV shows. They'll tell you what a struggle it is to stay upbeat, but it is nec-essary. They refuse to get down on themselves, no matter how often they hear no. They hang out with fellow actors and artists who experience the same thing and get sup-port from them. They remind themselves they are capa-ble, sometimes, like William Shatner, by accepting any role that comes along. Especially if they have suffered a long dry spell, they celebrate all opportunities to strut their stuff and contribute to their art.

They strengthen their spirits by asserting they're improving with each passing day.

They praise themselves for hanging in and not quitting long after less hardy souls have thrown in the towel.

They take inspiration from the stories of others that have broken through to conspicuous success. There are plenty of examples in practically every field.

California has one of the toughest bar exams in the country. If you want to practice law you have to overcome this mighty obstacle. When I was in law school, the passage rate was below 50 percent. Imagine making all of the sacrifices necessary for getting into school, paying for it for three or four years, passing all of your classes, and then failing the bar exam.

It gets worse. The bar exam is only offered twice each year, so you have to wait six months to take it again. When you do retake the test, there is no assurance you'll pass at that point.

Maxcy Filer was a Compton, California, fellow who flunked the bar not once or twice, but forty-seven times in a row. He started in 1967 but was not admitted to the bar till 1991. He had a son who went to law school and was admitted to practice long before his dad. Undaunted and unbowed, Maxcy persisted until he finally succeeded, and then he went on to practice for a number of years.

What did he tell himself over the course of over twenty-three years of exam taking without success?

"This time I'll make it!"

Sooner or later, he would be right, providing he didn't quit.

It might take you some time to earn exceptional money. But if you make it your unbending goal, you'll succeed as well.

This book is filled with shortcuts you can take and sharp moves you can make. I'm happy to share them, and I hope they work for you. After all, why make things hard if they can be easy?

But sometimes you need to earn more than you're worth by doing things the old-fashioned way—the hard way. If that's what it takes, so be it. Motivational speaker Les Brown says it this way: "Sure, it was hard, but you did it hard!"

Be prepared to take the slow road. And what is this when it comes to earning far more than you're worth?

It means talking a job at whatever wage and working your fanny off. Show up early. Stay late. Correct your own mistakes. Add far more value than is expected of you. Be enthusiastic. Stay upbeat. Sprinkle optimism and positive expectations about like Johnny Appleseed. When you're assigned too many tasks with short time frames, try to get things done anyway, on time and on target.

Never give up, and never say die.

Believe this, which will be as true for you as it has been for millions before you.

Start a job as an underpaid employee. Work hard anyway. You'll be paid more with time, and promotions will come your way, bringing even more rewards.

Keep pushing. Don't let up. As the years pass, your income will rise to the level of your contributions. Then, seemingly suddenly, you'll be paid far more than you're worth.

As I've already pointed out, CEOs make hundreds of times what the average worker earns. I've known and worked with many CEOs, often very capable individuals, and sometimes fine leaders. Are they worth hundreds of times what the average Joe or Josephine earns?

I think these folks, in private moments, would laugh if this question were presented to them, and in utter confidence they'd say, "No." They are paid far more than they're worth because at many prior career stages they added more value than they received. Finally, their income caught up to their competence. Then the income sprinted far ahead.

This can happen to you as well.

This is what I call the old-fashioned way of earning far more than you're worth. It boils down to having a quality frame of mind, a positive outlook toward what you do. Fall in love with your work, and it will love you back. It sounds like a fairy tale, but it is one that comes true!

Afterword

You Are Invited!

I've enjoyed sharing these tips with you for getting paid far more than you're worth. I realize they are a lot to take in, and you could feel a little overwhelmed.

I can help.

I coach a select group of folks who could use some help in positioning themselves to earn more. Send me a note or call me, and I'll share the details.

In the meantime, best of luck, and here's to your great success!

Gary S. Goodman, PhD, JD, MBA
President
The Goodman Organization, Inc.
garysgoodman@gmail.com
gary@negotiationschool.com
gary@drgarygoodman.com
(818) 970-GARY: (818) 970-4279